D1176452

strange movie full of death

scott wannberg

strange movie full of death

scott wannberg

Perceval Press

strange movie full of death
scott wannberg

ISBN 978-0-9819747-3-6
©2009 Perceval Press

Perceval Press
1223 Wilshire Blvd., Suite F
Santa Monica, CA 90403
www.percevalpress.com

Editor:
Henry Mortensen

Associate Editors:
Walter Mortensen
Viggo Mortensen

Design:
Michele Perez

Cover Photos:
Front: *Woodlawn* (detail) 2006
Back: *Topanga 36* (detail) 2003
Viggo Mortensen

Printed in Spain at Gráficas Jomagar S.L.

contents

introduction *peter case* **x**

strange movie full of death **xiii**

blues

depleted uranium boogaloo **1**

S. A. Griffin Two-Step **2**

Sad train depot blues **3**

a monster in every gas tank **4**

salt of the earth **5**

lost souls go down good with red wine **6**

barefoot summer **7**

jamboree **8**

the girl ran off **9**

if only **10**

lucky end of town **11**

say it ain't so **12**

lift up your throat **13**

end of day **14**

the last ride **15**

what you don't remember will be

    that much easier to forget **16**

sierra nobody **17**

Freedom Hotel **18**

911 **20**

vulnerable hotel **21**

no more funerals **22**

seen it coming **23**

tony scibella **24**

i think i've seen this movie somewhere before **25**

everything in its own time **26**

bobbing for poison apples can be

    hazardous to your health **27**

burning city **28**

we all need something **29**

Hootenanny **30**

lung city big kill **31**

once a bus **32**

odd river hoedown **33**

one more story **34**

there stands a house
   in memory of chris gaffney **35**

precarious underwear **36**

ambush boogaloo two-step **37**

must be a riot going on **38**

lonesome god blues **39**

death restoration blues **40**

Wounded River **41**

lunatic tunes **42**

gutless wonder **44**

eleven items or less **45**

i got lost **46**

liniment blues **48**

doorstop of love **50**

go fetch **52**

the eternal struggle **54**

sick ducks on ice **56**

wounds of love **59**

suicide river **61**

lowdown dirty shame **65**

politics

not that important **69**

Dead Man's Soiree **70**

habeas corpus hoedown **71**

south of any border **72**

Obama's Passport File **74**

drink it quick **75**

ginseng river **76**

Ugly Is as Ugly Does **77**

gutless love **78**

drowning prohibited by law **79**

my country 'tis of gutless thee **80**

point of no return **81**

purgatory yodel **82**

lunch meat of the poor **83**

hoedown **84**

refreshing bakery of the heart **85**

for the life of me **86**

ways and means **87**

you bet your ass **88**

safe harbor **89**

hanging in there **90**

traffic jam **92**

Phone Call at 3 A.M. **93**

undone **94**

mañana american eagle **95**

out west, somewhere **96**

negligent **97**

state of something union **98**

late at night **99**

appeasement blues **100**

rap to 2009 **101**

michele bachmann blues rag **104**

traces of human **105**

underdeveloped utopia hoedown **107**

hope in a bottle **110**

slums of gold **112**

bush legacy tour hallucination raga **114**

the day after **115**

frankenstein meets rod blagojevich **117**

bobby in the box **119**

evidence kit full of anything you need to get by **120**

the mean streets of love **122**

jubilee **124**

recovery

traveling **129**

that old burning sensation **130**

the house love built **131**

the road to recovery **132**

there was this time **133**

there is a radiance **134**

they're burning down the dance hall **135**

everybody **136**

earth shall come knocking **137**

hurt city **138**

rags to riches **139**

emergency room of the stars **140**

take your things inside **141**

dakota lunch meat **142**

satisfied feeling **143**

crank her up **144**

this prison sure be fine **145**

roll me over **146**

a storm might be coming **147**

weary river **148**

wunderkind park **149**

Roast Beef Kill **150**

where to go when your favorite hospital gets sick **152**

one night fits all **154**

bye-bye sun **156**

holding cell of love **158**

down and out **159**

let everybody come in **161**

moodswing hotel **164**

what i want for my 56th birthday **166**

luminous possibility **168**

introduction

This book is a guide to survival in the twenty-first century. It is a labor-saving device.

Scott is a singer. There are no chords to his songs, just the Truth, aloft in musical rolling tongues designed to bring down the roof and walls, from Alphabet City to Zebulon, Tennessee, via the Strother Martin Memorial Freeway of Love.

God has a universal health plan sewed into his forehead.
All you got to do is rub yours against his.

His methods are sound, man. He can walk through the walls whenever he feels like it, and that's every evening. He can talk to anyone about absolutely everything, and does, daily. He makes time stop and look at itself, if only until the next news flash, the next uncoiling national disaster, the next prison breakout, then he sets 'em up again. Kaboom!

Just like Bukowski, or Dante, for that matter, Scott stays up late watching the all-night movie in his heart, all the while scribbling math notes, death threats, and love songs to God and Man on big sheets of unruled paper, taking dictation from the ether, never pausing for anything short of breath. And now it's all here in this little book, his latest, maybe greatest fortune cookies for the hope-impaired, his limber language climbing towers and jumping down barricades, his pen an uncanny divining rod for Living Water, his jokes ripping the cosmos a new one.

I went down and out to find gold under the asphalt.
I beat my chest and sang like a mockingbird.

How does he know so much?
there's a musician in your heart
he may not be up to it
but he's the only one left

He's got the full kit. Acute societal observation:
the sun's left the party but you're still on fire.
bring in the cool people
let them show you how to relax.

Prophecy:
Soon all the chairs will be turned upside down.
The wine will return to water.

The Higher Power makes numerous appearances:
God carries a super-huge gun
when he goes into dangerous neighborhoods.

The essential coin of his realm is the hilarious razor-sharp line. Like diamond bullets blazing through your forehead, he's on his way to the head of the river to terminate Brando/Kurtz with extreme diction. The wiseguy from your third-grade class is here, a thousand years later, wide awake and walking on clouds of poison radiation, skipping over rings of satellite trash, undaunted, ecstatic in the Laundromat, getting free sodas out of the Coke machine and giving them away to passersby, a genius double-talking in parables. The garbage man pulls up, and he's got a heart of gold, hauling it all away, idolized by youngsters when his truck breaks down, kind beyond reason to canines and kids, surgically dissecting the blowhards of the eternal present line by line, breath by breath.

Scott's a hero of mine, the fastest mind in town, the hippest tongue, a spontaneous fountain that washes the bomb dust and bloodstains off what's left of the world, carrying a message of hope in a disintegrating cosmos:

my wounds aren't all that special
we all got to go down
don't matter in which order
that soft-shoe just might kill you
count your fingers and toes
no matter what answer you get
it'll be the right one.

Peter Case
2009

strange movie full of death

Strange movie full of death
asks us to play ourselves
as the front door falls face first
onto the floor.
Women and men explore consent
in the back alley
where memoirs get written
between gunshots.
Smiling zombies in police lineups of love
look painfully familiar.
The ER is overfull,
and First Class is on fire.
I went down and out to find gold under the asphalt.
I beat my chest and sang like a mockingbird.
The ambulance is coming to see you
and the murder rate has its own new hour show on HBO.
Beneath the bleeding stairs
an uneasy truce is reached,
and lovers intend to do their laundry
before the next attack.

blues

depleted uranium boogaloo

rasha abbas age 15 leukaemia
dhamia qassem age 13 acute leukaemia
address this song bleeding moon
ashwark hamid age 13 acute leukaemia
oulah falahd age 4 kidney tumor
tareq abdullah age 13 acute leukaemia
call god collect and who picks up the tab
abdul kadem modushed 36 leukaemia
karrar abdul emir leukaemia
ahmed walid chronic myeloid leukaemia
zeinab manwar 15 leukaemia
jawab hassan 55 cancer of the stomach
amal hassan saleh 21 cancer
linger in the quiet room
your love abides
bodies cry
soon the sleep
soon, soon, wounded
tune, soon.

1

S. A. Griffin Two-Step

The sun shines in your back door someday.
We sang loud in the Aleutians.
Sky divers have your poems written in their skin.
Diana Bonebrake sings and we
walk backward up a mountain range.
The medicine bag is full of dancing men and women.
Permission to climb aboard.
For whatever ails you
we got it.
The highway has no press agent
and rubs our stomach as we glide North
toward epiphany and damn right.
God is a sumo wrestler attempting to lose weight.
Dreams have their own political party,
and you can tell the border guards your real name.
The sun shines in your front door someday.
We sing wherever we will have us.

Sad train depot blues

All the weary brain cells elope with leaking hearts in
the holy 99-Cent Store where ongoing attempts at
empathy and love are learning to stand up for themselves
and be recognized.
The irritable weather bends down to pat my hair
and teach me licks. Lonely women and men
slowly walk back and forth in the alley of
lost passports. I heard that the dinner was edible
and people who meant well could actually be allowed
to sing, even if off key. Pain left its forwarding
address on your forehead and the luxury boxes
are full of mannequins with large stupid grins.
There are rooms in which hearing doesn't matter.
You simply lean against the wall and find yourself
still in the game. I lost track of anything resembling time.
Soothsayers get stuck to flypaper and their predictions are
open for interpretation. The head surgeon's only question
is, can you dance? I somersault over barbed wire
in search of the next big deal. Can you find me in
all this smoke? Hello, I think I love you.
I didn't come to hurt you. Sad train rounding
the bend on my lap. Glow calm in insurrection
night. So many simultaneous wars at work. Find me
human, in the moment, on fire with life.

3

a monster in every gas tank

something in the mattress makes it hard to sleep
i wish somebody here could pronounce words
monsters in every gas tank
all of them, if you allow it, will tell you the same
story
between fantasy's idea of reality
the houses shake along the road
can we become comfortable?
upstairs in the back of my head
the plumbing once in awhile works
all of my brothers
share the same name
it makes it easy when the lights break
got to tiptoe, quicksand on debonair toes
tell the DP to adjust the lights
how long until the next load?
liars not doing all that well
monsters want to be young too
a long time sometimes goes by way too fast
i barely can make out your headlights
sway on this precarious ledge with me for a bit
king daddy jazz in every eye
blood transfusions need sleep too
love falls naked from the sky
a monster dreams in every tank
the houses keep shaking on the side of your road.

4

salt of the earth

On the Execution of the Week channel
I see someone that looks suspiciously like me
being led to the gallows.
Sultry middle-aged women
carrying big weapons
march up and down my street
trying to keep the neighborhood from exploding.
The choir intended to arrive at 5 A.M.
but their bus got grabbed by a giant ape.
The sick-looking guy in the right corner
would have you believe he knows where the money lives.
You're too thin, the hired killer said,
on his way to becoming a new currency.
I called Dixie collect,
told her to sell.
She said, maybe later.
The salt of the earth makes my coffee frown.
Love, barefoot and bleeding,
waits for you in the Greyhound lobby.
Soon the tender season might arrive.
Hang on.
Keep all fingers inside the vehicle and crossed.
Death said, please read my book.
As soon as the light gets out of jail.

lost souls go down good with red wine

durability does not mean ramming your head repeatedly
into a solid wall
you might not even look all that good doing it.
those who have confess they truly desire to love
those who ain't got will be over on time
the buildings these days grow tall and scary
watch where your feet choose to live
something hard at work in the soil
lovers must be back by eleven
my name was Stay Out All Night
then we all got new clothes
and a hard-to-read email from the big man
all that getup on the horse
someday soon will have to find a way to get down.
prime time has a hole in its foot.
go fetch the podiatrist
gold got found up north
lost souls go down good with red wine
i'll crawl through your window soon
i need to figure my longitude and latitude
hours and hours of prairie.

barefoot summer

brokedown men and women claim heartily they'll
survive the next phase of the war that never seemingly
ends, it's just a matter of time and barefoot summer
waltzing through shrapnel and minefields.
when your cold bones rattle
when your head yearns to explode
take a deep breath
and hop the barefoot summer freight
up the bleeding line
to the next move of the wounded heart
where brokedown men and women
crawl unanimously toward a healing
where you quench the thirst
and relearn your name.
when the world claims it will never get you
when the specialists vow whatever you got is yours for
keeps, i invite you to the party that we are
struggling every day against the shit.
i ask for your backbeat.
i might not be able to do it in tune
but i'll hum it proud regardless.
we are all broken down at times
and sometimes the steps keep adding on.
no particular hurry. one damn step at a time.
going to catch the barefoot summer local.
going to roll on down to your campfire's ways and means.
every kind of vocal range.
every type of instrument.
when your heart fractures a few inches
when your eyes finally relax and truly begin seeing,
barefoot summer will ask you to call collect.

jamboree

FDR's polio did not steal his voice
he's in the jamboree
where mountains slept
earth went to school
earth said, who goes there?
not much, said the jamboree
where does weather go to have fun?
did you hear the one about the fat lady?
no, sang the i-meant-well folks
it's got a fierce rhythm, said jamboree
where people met themselves
repeatedly
until no scripts were needed
i want to live on any island, said jamboree
can't you be more specific? the clock mumbled
i don't believe in terror, the girl scout smiles
how many cattle did you say?
there's room in my sleeves for you, hummed jamboree
got to go now with my trustworthy broom
lots of bones to sweep up
there's gonna be some party come morning
we stand in the middle of the street
everything is just one second too wide
don't matter
we give what we can
earth has a boyfriend
earth has a girlfriend
i don't make friends any too easy, snarled the world
jamboree leapt onto earth's back
good morning.

the girl ran off

the girl ran off with the monster
they struck each other with a smile
the monster's first book glowed in the dark
death wanders barefoot
claiming he can't help loving them young
the girl will one day be a woman
the monster loves the oboe
soon the comfortable beds
soon your mortgage
death builds a tree house in the backyard
then forgets the address
everybody someday will have a name
roll the dice of the blind
roll them serene
the girl changes her name twice a week
just keeping you on your toes
soon the dam begins to crack
hope the water that'll drown you tastes good.

if only

if only Custer had decided to take the Gatling guns.
he was too locked up in his own peculiar step.
maybe it wouldn't of mattered.
Sitting Bull and Crazy Horse were out to kick some ass.
if only God hadn't of been vacationing in Hiroshima
when the *Enola Gay* came calling.
he might have agreed to see you.
his manager will have to suffice.
tell the thirsty people to pray for rain.
if only they'd put the mail in the right boxes.
the mailman needs reading glasses.
the world's funniest man
lost his timing.
if only they sold dark beer.
stay out of the sun.
it's looking for someone to burn.

lucky end of town

the slave trade swore it ended.
but there's a lot of silence on the work floor.
let's unroll our mighty big plan
on paper that will never burn.
dogs will be dogs
in certain moments.
the hardnoses want to move in.
i got a spare room in my head.
i'm too empathetic to do them any good.
you get solid bed rest
in the lucky end of town.
the master of ceremonies can't speak all that well
we'll have to pay special attention to his body
movement.
the poker game's been going for hours
at the most relaxed table in the lucky end of town.
before morning some will have lost legs and arms.
god got awful sick but no emergency room would bother
as he didn't have insurance.

say it ain't so

say it ain't so
as the big bloody rock lands on my biodegradable
dumb-ass head
soothsayers roam the alley
jazz in every pore
no beheadings
time's one big blur
say you got it made
as the sun disappears
we're carded at the door by people who once thought
it'd be fun to know us
make a left turn
get that hole in one
get that boulder rolled up the hill
tonight it's swing
i left my history at the hatchecker's
move over, god
this is your pal befuddled
monsters in the toy store
a long drop down.

lift up your throat

there's a fire burning in the heart
nobody knows where it lives
we'll have to look for smoke
the fire departments of the world
are dreaming
there's a landscape in the heart
torn and forgotten
a thin man lives there
and he swears he wants to learn the holy city of music
toward morning all seems the same
lift up your throat
there's a book being talked about
maybe we are pages in it
there might even be pictures
i heard the wise man was ghostwriting
all kinds taken here
there's a government running naked through debris
this government swears it will run the marathon
only it disappeared during mile 15
lift up your face
follow the highways there
toward the dubious house of silence
there's a musician in your heart
he may not be up to it
but he's the only one left
they come now with the death list
if only they knew how to spell.

end of day

home says it's time you came back to it.
too many nameless days swing in wide arcs.
the posse rode out looking for love.
that love runs very fast and does not trust anyone.
the head of the family waddles up to the edge
begins to hum.
home wrote a letter
claiming it was too young to serve.
you sweat too good at end of day.
the sun's left the party but you're still on fire.
bring in the cool people
let them show you how to relax.
the cool people are on strike
they demand better wages and some understanding.
pretend we're on our own
and the band remembers our requests.
the judges do not like black robes anymore.
they're going through the catalogue now
picking out a new color.
the on-duty sentries are yawning.
end of day drives up
smirking.
we nod to ourselves with grace.
put out your hands, palm up
get ready to make a catch.

the last ride

come running quick
there's a fire that demands putting out
strobe lights live in god's beard
vulnerable days irritable nights
i'll have a large cup to go
man came forward
man done gone asunder
dig deep for treasure
how long can a man howl?
the last ride forming in the quad
who will secretly sing with me?
across the catechism of the dark side of the moon
thin ladies and their ongoing rotund friends
all take part in the special
come humming or just come
the heart will find you
man shot himself out of a cannon
the new age drunkenly weaves
the heart knows which side of the floor
you get up from
bring in the food
the fire got burnt out
please give it a drink
the horses all know where you live.

what you don't remember will be
that much easier to forget

count how many heads you got at end of day
can your heart take it?
i hear the piranha are biting
the police know me by my first name
sometimes the load gets a little too heavy
it's a long way to the well
the water better be worth it
what you don't remember
will be that much easier to forget
the dead, the dying
they moved away
to a more healthy climate
the last sniper in the world
just got gun shy
the mâitre d's teeth are sharp
pawnshops on parade
my wounds aren't all that special
we all got to go down
don't matter in which order
that soft-shoe just might kill you
count your fingers and toes
no matter what answer you get
it'll be the right one.

sierra nobody

the girl's name is sierra nobody
dogs let her pet them
phases of something like a moon
all of us can't be undone
hot food on the premises
bring your kill home
the vice-president has eerie feelings in his eye
highway patrol might be here any minute
they quiver and quake
government leaking blood
gimme a working band-aid
here comes the kid with the lie-detector set
he looks buff
jack and jill ran out of hills
fetch me a tale
the story sometimes moves slow
all those offers to dance
piñatas of stone.

Freedom Hotel

God carries a super-huge gun
when he goes into dangerous neighborhoods.
Love woke up this morning with a nasty headache.
The hospitals are overflowing.
Go about your Earth tenderly.
God has a universal health plan sewed into his
forehead.
All you got to do is rub yours against his.
Pain just checked into Freedom Hotel,
the place you call home
The number of soldiers returning from Iraq
who are suicidal has risen.
God cannot bless America
as he claims no favorites with
so many other countries.
Support the troops, yelled the blind sentry,
bumping into walls made of glass.
Support them to come home and wind up living on the
street
or in health facilities that aren't properly equipped
to treat them.
John McCain, who should know better,
is against the new GI Bill.
Love woke up this morning with a 102-degree
temperature.
Go among the hurt people with empathy.
Don't demand too much blood because frankly
there's not all that much left.
The musical selection for tonight
is discordant.
The janitor is sweeping up bone matter.
Can you tell me in which room of the Freedom Hotel
I can find the heart?

Is there a speech we can hear that will explain
away the slow dying?
I will take you by your shaking hand
and lead you across the bleeding dance floor.
Freedom Hotel claims the evening belongs to us.
Nobody can tell us what the morning will bring.
God has many bodyguards
and they all run on rage.
The headlines are torn.
The news is ragged and on life support.
Soon all the chairs will be turned upside down.
The wine will return to water.
Go slow, sidestep land mines.
If we are capable of making it to the roof of
Freedom Hotel
a comfortable bed will find us.
The elevator broke.
There are hundreds of stairs to maneuver.
We put one hopeful foot in front of the reluctant
other.
If we make it, we'll give you a call.
If we make it, we'll throw a party.

911

911 was a very good year.
the 13th day of christmas got out of jail.
romance worked retail.
i came here to sing something dumb.
i came here to attest to my stupidity.
the marching armies have bad feet.
podiatry, maybe.
executioners younger every day.
please do my back.
the stairs here are a bitch.
president bush went hunting with vice-president cheney
one of them came back.
could be SOS
could be that wake-up call.
dance on the table
tell them who and what you are.
drive the getaway car, baby
lend me your hand.

vulnerable hotel

sole survivors of some strange new dance
line up in alleys full of broken bottles and bones.
the commander-in-insanity coughs up blood
in preparing his state of disarray speech.
quiet now is your ongoing process of pain.
the plainclothes squad loses its ability to dress.
the vulnerable hotel at the end of the
alligator's mouth
has a light in the window naming you and me.
i carry my school on top of my hair to amuse
the blind watchdogs.
the next dance just might remember
our forwarding address.
it was touch and go for awhile in the emergency room
but the doctor has now taken off his clothes and
claims his body is a new planet.
beauty is subjective, the ugly lover sang
and the war is wearing a condom tonight
in order to escape paternity suits.
i hung upside down from a chandelier in
order to caress gravity.
the vulnerable hotel climbs into bed
and its dreams are on fire.

no more funerals

the last funeral in the world
can't remember its name
the city's got a migraine
walk soft
so much quicksand everywhere
the music's pretty fucking good
the firing squad is taking its time
the last victim in the world
is sleeping in this morning
open a window wide
let that pain in
our hearts scrape the walls
we'll sing it so loud their ears might break
we'll sing it and go on down
alive, wounded, and on fire.

seen it coming

the ambulance is speeding, claims it loves you
should of seen it coming, the blind guy testified
his testimony could be tossed
i'm hearing all kinds of voices
a lot of empty space between my ears
the tender people on the endangered species list
tell all bartenders your story
they've seen them all before
only survivors entitled to limos
we need a green thumb
at the end of another long one
so easy to argue
a man and woman will see it coming
the three pigs warned the wolf about the dangers of
huffin' and puffin'
not in my lifetime
water's rising
i hope you weren't lying when you said you could swim.

tony scibella

he invents honky-tonk
you can tell time by the way he dances
his address is the moment
the adventures of tony and s.a. in amsterdam
for all ages
black ace skyline
who's that masked man?
just tony
playing piano boogie
come, listen
he teaches dance
all the singing a human can be
his backbeat a yes.

i think i've seen this movie somewhere before

quasimodo and the belle of amherst
canvass the neighborhood
god is up for reelection
stretch those muscles, honey
a fool can be divine
the doctor has a big black bag
don't hold the fort too long
splinters will crawl into your fingers
the party is packing up
the next county needs him bad
take old men dancing
temperature gauge broke
put your skin where your mouth once lived
the hard-of-hearing referees
are roaming the dark end of the alley
the getaway car just had twins
i think i've seen this movie somewhere before
a cast of thousands
actually it was the same actor
cloned a thousand times
here come the chimpanzees
they be laughing shrilly
they just came from the rose garden
the doctor's nurse looks a bit pale
she went into the woods
the music she made.

everything in its own time

lunatics in the coffeepot
deadbeats economics experts
when does the reckoning come down?
that rarified air gets trapped in your throat
a pretty good hunch
claims it's hopefully free
meaty dogs trip over their leashes
all in a rush to be seen
everything in its own time
the soda jerk smiled
i'd like to go home with two of everything
the water really intends to rise
they got a warrant out for god's arrest
seems he also uses the pen name satan
i reinvent myself daily
the tornado said
he meant it, i think
takes nine men to play baseball
hope it's a day game on real grass
lunatics in the bottom line
rogue planets need not apply
i saw your x-ray the other day
who would of thunk
twirl your baby
everything in its own time
the duck waddled
heavens to betsy
and if her name isn't betsy
she still needs to be on time.

bobbing for poison apples can be hazardous to your health

the wicked witch of every known geopolitical corner
has trouble with her wisdom teeth
she's very afraid of dentists everywhere
something about her mother and a drill
you don't want to park your car in such a garage
bobbing for poison apples can be hazardous
to your health
prince charming's rap sheet goes back for hours
your hair will stand up on your head when you
give it a read
they got valet parking in hell
i think it was you who ran up at me
asked me if i could recall what the weather will
soon be like
man, i gave that up years ago
i work the matinees now and then
holding up a see-through bag full of snarling people
heart attacks in every pore
the waitress can only hold up so many plates
i'd like this next lick to go to . . .
we're almost to the end of this godforsaken excuse
of a hall
what was that room number again?

burning city

the city went to bed with itself
you could hear arguing through the walls all night
long
the pundits have a name for all of this
they just stupidly left it on the side of the road
men of irrefutable action suddenly freeze as if
covered in cement
not everyone can be an action figure
you need to climb a dumb-ass mountain
that goes on for years
when you finally reach the top
the lights will hurt your eyes
the city burns three times a day
the latter two are reruns for those who just got to
know
sometimes the hour seemingly gets late
sometimes the day just disappears
the city took a contract out on itself
maybe the police need to know
which one of us can speak their language?
holy man wanders onto a land mine
land mine says you become guts just like anyone else
come quick momma, bring the iodine
tell the army to call it due to rain
the city eats its tail
a little short on self-discipline
but oh that wonderful savory taste.

we all need something

lock down your heart
enemy at the door.
some rumor about free food.
we all need something to see us through.
esoteric people search the trashbins
looking for what's on tonight's agenda.
god went to stretch and discovered arthritis.
he's wandering the cheap end of town
trying to get pain medicine.
the conga players show up, finally
mumbling something about a recession.
all i thought i needed was a place to fall.
sometimes the distance is that great.
sometimes it's not too far at all.
let me siphon some of your brain.
i'd really appreciate being able to see straight.
we all need something to hold us dear.
the earth retracts a little bit each day.
one war quietly ends and a brand-new one begins.
some days all those wars turn into one another.
promise me i'll halfway look good when the firing
squad finally lands.
some days kiss your retreating spirit
there's no sense denying it.
radio doesn't feel like working.
talk to me in a language i can feel.
love scratches at the door.
it's wounded, can't remember much.
open up your body
a new country is being born there.
maybe it's a country we can carry on our back.
maybe it will dream us.
the enemy at the door forgot who it was fighting.

Hootenanny

Hootenanny's gums bleed easy.
Best you learn to floss your brain.
Matinee idols self-implode
as the sun lights a cigarette and begins to weave.
The recovery room is locked up tight,
while the last bottle of wine is making
all the right moves.
Hootenanny burst its appendix
and the table of contents is full of screaming.
Vulnerable talk-show hosts lose their ability
to speak,
and all outlaws must report in to their
parole officers
by midnight.
Hate asks you to lunch
and the prisoner exchange just got cancelled.
Hootenanny rubs its bleeding belly
and asks you to stand up.
So many lovers
and only one bullet left.

lung city big kill

kiss my everloving what the fuck,
said the pacifist.
i got tremors in me.
okay, sang american psychiatry.
lung city big kill
is the name of the main feature.
i recognize the lead.
once empathy answered the door,
now it's anybody's game.
would you shimmy with me in the dark?
i'd do anything in the dark, if you'd name all seven
dwarves.
listen to the wind.
it asks our hair where we live.

once a bus

once a bus kissed new mexico
i slept on the wind
cap'n. g. steered
the ongoing hillbillies hovered in the dark
once a bus stood on two legs
claimed i can fly
i rode with such an outfit once
the streets of santa fe can become dangerously narrow
we walked through taco bell's drive-through
hillbillies evaporated
an idiot and his whip
pick a card . . . any card
we walked the santa fe night
sweated out all our wild turkey bourbon
once a bus had children
the open road our biography and lunch
still claim i can fly
let the atmosphere clear
one of these hundreds of years
i saw you guys in 1989
sometimes the sea is clean
sometimes the show goes on
once a bus kicked off its shoes
your lead.

odd river hoedown

everyone's favorite dog is seriously considering
going rabid.
do you know any good trial lawyers?
a new day coming, the hired guns promise.
spineless congress limped off and died.
i eat you, says the executive branch, and spit you out.
old-timers rush toward the fountain of youth.
nobody to home, captain.
the engine room's been deserted.
they all got naked and headed north toward odd river.
you dive in and become a new planet.
the knife whistles down
missing your neck by inches.
must be pledge break.
send me your hearts and letters.
going to finally make the big getaway.
going to blend in.
quit pulling the cord.
odd river drinks my feet.
gonna balance twelve plates on my head
one for every day of christmas.
if truth be known
god is irish.
i've seen the film.
the weight of the world sometimes gets boring.
we'll try and rewrite it
as soon as we become uncrushed.

one more story

the beautiful couple came to my place
they thought i was somebody else
they were so beautiful
you could go blind staring at them
missing persons came to my door
asked if i was grounded
i live in a village of skin
one more story for all the roads
make it a single malt scotch
have i got a story for you
one more story before i got born
the beautiful couple oohed and aahed
all you got to do is let the dust settle
animals who love
those incorrigible unpredictable elastic people
shape-shifting at rush hour every day
one more story to hold up the bookshelf
the hard couple came to my place the next day
they damn well knew me
your mind could snap
in such heat
quite a lot of miles left to go
bring me home.

there stands a house
in memory of chris gaffney

for dave alvin

the radios here are quiet
the movie almost ended but the screenwriter came
running in
wanted to add more
love got a day job
might even get home before the sun disappears
there stands this house
that knows many languages
a resonance will land on your doorstep
asking you to greet it barefoot
on balconies of snow
the dancing girls are writing memoirs
there is a heart
holding up the earth
there is a soiree
rolling uphill
rise now and let your inflections steer you
chris gaffney, poet, storyteller, captain of the ship
rides all the high countries
the radios begin to get out of jail
they raise their playlists to the sun
love's working the night shift
a rhythm will move into your house
it knows your height and width
there are landing lights on the dark side of the moon
there are footprints in the moment
bring your all night nuance
one irrefutable foot in front of the other
chris gaffney, oxygen, empathy, ways and means
there stands a house
the earth sleeps in
when it needs air.

precarious underwear

altitude's attitude leaves a lot to be desired
the king and queen are joined at the hip
in the house of fading memory
mirrors study themselves
the policemen are a shade unsound
precarious underwear is no guarantee against
the freeze
summer demands to be heard
god slipped in the bathroom and cut open the back
of his head
fortunes of war for the asking in every outhouse
quick, throw a rug on that hardwood floor
dreamers hanging from trees
we desperately need some outlaws
feel that music?
we go bump in the night
islands doing time in a sea of little mercy.

ambush boogaloo two-step

smallpox one day will be big
every boy becomes tab hunter
the juke joints implode with burning valor
the second coming soon to be at this theater
bring the whole crew
papa rolls in some very strange matter
it kills his itch
momma is hearing things in the water
she might be pretty on her money
that water takes longer and longer to freeze
man from outer space shrugged at me
i said, give me two on the left side
father time just shot himself by accident
he was just doing his ambush boogaloo two-step
best know the names of all the players
your roll is coming up soon.

must be a riot going on

death is hiring a new campaign manager
somebody who's very well read
the sentries are losing their touch
the rain intends to stay awhile
play that down-home music
say your damn name
must be a riot going on
nobody really needs to be blamed
you climb the big ugly bike
you pedal as fast as a hurricane
all i need is a place to flop
some good drinking whiskey
death is learning how to dance
its legs are a long time coming.

lonesome god blues

god got lonely
went looking for anybody that would talk
god wanted to somehow atone for george bush
nobody was buying
there was a hootchie dancer, though
who told time right
she began to sing
the clouds didn't part but the ride was comfortable
god tried to figure where it all went wrong
all watches were synchronized
the clowns land
try and create laughter
some of them died smiling
god wound up on *american idol*
trying to blend in
the cheap seats caught fire
dancers to the left
the king and queen of bullshit
receive guests all night long
their liquor is good.

death restoration blues

death is getting a makeover today.
it wanted to appear young, vital, alive.
only the best doctors are in attendance.
i was hanging upside down
trying to mind nobody's business.
death claimed i was its best pal,
that all its tricks came from me.
i shiver a bit and begin to sing in a tongue
that has no reference to anything breathing.
the thin pale faces of lost love
crowd in through the windows of my eyes
and i cannot refuse the harsh music
that slides in beneath locked doors.
death is claiming it won the lottery
and the hotel management is empathetic
and will not kick it out into the street.
death coos soft lies into my ears.
i find myself in agreement
and stumble in the dark
holding what is left of my own.

Wounded River

Dead men do not enunciate all that good.
Hearts hang low on a strong-enough line.
Pain brushes its teeth and begins to grin.
God used to have office hours.
Now we are on our own.
I feel your fear when you say your name aloud.
Wounded River is writing our autobiography.
Lovers become nervous.
Can you still scream in key?
Sing one, darling,
sing one in key.
Blood lives in the food
that swears it's edible.
Blind men and women
buy tickets for the afternoon matinee.
Something in the telling of the story.
Something in the broken bone.
Wounded River baptizes us
in languages not yet born.

lunatic tunes

shake your troubled tired true-blue body
shake your ability to encompass and enhance
inhale the ways and means of the moment
they got broken idioms being spoke from the dance floor
not quite the dictionary you claimed you were capable
of editing
get your own personal trainer
they come in on the midnight train
lunatic tunes in every sixth box of wheaties
blind cathy will lead us in prayer
pat her head tender as you place your tithe in the jar
god has a really good layaway plan
an easy-enough
prison sentence awaits around the corner
the warden, an unrepentant devotee of musical theater
makes it mandatory for prisoners on their way to be
executed
to sing their favorites
the winner, "stairway to heaven"
place your broken face against the frosty glass
your rapidly turning-blue face
can sometimes smile
we used to form complete sentences once
in a time when language had fun
nowadays grunts pass for exposition
the most erudite of us
fallen back to rudimentary sign language
when asked my opinion of how the world works
i tear off my clothes and howl
this boy has something to say!
the producers nod
what i'm trying to make them understand is,
i truly need to shit

you are so passionate, they agree,
you should be the one
you will be the one who leads us home
i went home recently
the doors were locked
the rent had doubled
the war went on all around us
it seemed to be having a good time
the war, don't you know, gave us rent money
don't ever be shy, it said
we walk up and down the main boulevard
marking our territory
the beautiful people seem younger with each
passing moment
the beautiful people seem immune
i'd go ahead and shoot one to see if it's really so
but i lost my gun in the last head to head
never did like how they felt in my hand
never wanted the pain they put in my head
the national anthems of all the countries concerned
lunatic tunes seeking a parole contract
when patsy cline tells me she's crazy
i'm right there, sitting in her lap
this is how the theater allows you to sit, comfortable
this is where we'll be come the 7th-inning stretch.

gutless wonder

the gutless wonder just landed
it's taking heavy casualties
i'd like to engage it
but i left my teeth back at the bank
the gutless wonder never needs to nick itself shaving
as its beard self-perpetuates
the gutless wonder knows your debit card PIN number
in a cheap-enough motel room
on some highway in need of an infrastructure facelift
something holy is undertaken
put candles in the window
pray for rain
the drought needs a drink
the homicide guys need to solve something soon
big joe turner sings why don't my dog bark when you
come around
ask him when he's finished gnawing on his rawhide
he'll level with you
the gutless wonder is making eyes at me
it asked if i needed my neck rubbed
maybe once i get it out of this rope.

eleven items or less

idiots snap to attention when i pass
tell the crowd to keep its minimum below a roar
i just graduated from try-harder university
some mongrel cur ate my diploma
eleven items or less will set you free
the warden promises to look another way
don't let the cops give you a speeding ticket
i tossed a rock into the bottom of the wishing well
it took one hour and twenty seconds to get there
i don't mind wasting time
it's all i really have
i'd just love to spend some of it with you
i've certainly got no plan to save the world any time soon
the traffic keeps getting worse
could you swing by and pick me up at eight?
i sat up late last night on the edge of my chair
i waited for an epiphany
i heard fingers on a chalkboard
writing a poignant SOS
the republicans and democrats were seen in the armory
drawing their weapons and ammo
i hope the ensuing party is what everyone expected
god just got his own atomic bomb
someone talk with him until he decides to blow.

i got lost

i got lost
forgot my name
i self-arrested myself
didn't like the way i looked back at me from the mirror
i ran into a thick brick wall
it felt so good
the planet's on fire
i could drink something
there's old horror hidden in every new package
i came here to testify
but my right hand is now glued to an overrated bible
i came here to surf
but the waves disappeared
you tell me you ran into god on the street
you tell me he's an old black blues guy
how do you know?
couldn't god be the guitar and not the man?
the chicken and the egg are slugging it out to see who
came first
i couldn't care less as i get to go last

i'd like to finish checking in, get a room with a
comfortable bed
but the desk clerk keeps finding more paperwork
i need to fill out
at this rate my pen will run out of ink
or i will
the coast might one day be truly clear
unless it falls into the ocean
the monsters are lonesome
they whimper and sob
we've made it to the end of the trail
but our feet just won't say no
don't you dare panic

try to not unglue
somebody's coming soon to ask you out
you'll be finally going home
in eden everyone gets their own personal tote bag
to throw up in
the bus is leaving in a few minutes
i packed you a lunch
it might not be fit to eat
but it looks hefty
when you get to the border
you'll have to go through the story we prepared
one more time
don't bite off more than you can absorb
i'll be waiting for your eventual return
i'll be sitting on this bar stool
it took years for me to find it
i don't need to go anywhere anymore
nobody would have me
my bones are ornery
my capacity for self-punishment at an all-time high
tell everyone i once loved them
tell everyone i might one day again care
they got a mediocre pianist here five nights a week
the way she plays is just about all i can handle right now.

liniment blues

quick baby sister, run and get the liniment
daddy's muscles are about to explode
the astronauts keep landing their modules in your
daddy's head
it's getting ornery with life there
soon we'll take that vacation
soon a new language will embrace us
there's a price on daddy's head
the government clerks mumble all day
when night comes they begin to snap
i'm walking in circles on the playground
i'm trying to keep a date
the sanitation boys are a bit overcome by a sudden
increase in garbage
the haunted house is now on the market
the association fees a mite high
quick baby sister, swear it ain't so
daddy's hands go wherever they want
the god he hangs with is getting more erratic each day
the cell phone that was to have set us free just took a
bullet
a damp box full of negligent possibility
the cold front is rumored soon
will you be ready?
the old bluesmen
they have their own words for this condition
all the specialists in the world
and then some
they draw sticks
some lucky one will make it to the show
somebody's always preparing to leave
but the door never gets made
miles and miles across the living-room carpet

anything can happen
they found a body floating in the beef stew
did you know him?
quick baby sister, just try to save my soul
it ain't worth much and what little is left is on fire
daddy's walking barefoot to congress
he's gonna lay down the law
none of the tourists ever pull up alongside him
nobody is curious enough to check him out
some fine unregretful morning
all your painstaking exercise will pay off
quick baby sister, put another slug into my résumé
the roadhouse up ahead takes all ages
i might be back sometime come morning
if i'm not there
you know how i talk.

doorstop of love

put the cold wind in your back pocket
it won't be necessary for our little chat
humorous men and women are disappearing with alacrity
the parking tickets keep going up
the next dance supposedly was ours
but the bandleader gave us a very odd look
the doorstop of love allows the sun to enter
inhale that fresh air if it doesn't make you sick
the cold mornings come and inevitably go
two strangers sharing body heat beneath the floodlights
what little it takes to upend the applecart
down here in the street everyone claims to be casanova
the way you enter a room
the way you sing those awful songs you bought into
makes my cantankerous ears actually listen
does anyone truly ever know anyone else?
every home is a potential missing persons office
the homeless orchestra sees us coming
they pull their instruments out of the gutter
and begin to cut loose
in the deaf new morning of still one more day
that may or may not be kind to us
don't hurt me, you say, i don't want any more hurt
i'm no doctor, i say, but i will go slow
the statute of liberties eventually runs out
bring me your wounded and torn
the hearts pumping in the pawnshop windows
they will be redeemed soon
a lucid-enough idea man once claimed
the human race was an amphorous mess
we row our leaky canoe back and forth
across the life-sustaining water
there's an island with our name on it

somewhere hidden in this fog
we're damaged goods
in some kind of hootenanny rehab
when i touch you
the locked gate blows wide open
when you touch me
i remember how to move
the city is crowded with emergency rooms
full of lovers who slipped over each other's feet
the nurses begin to sing our names
they must have been in on the rehearsal
put the war back in its box
it won't need to sit in
we are nothing more than imperfect human beings
searching for the not-alone
it takes a long time sometimes to get there
sometimes alone is very persuasive
pour a shot of good single malt scotch
toast all infections leaving office
the king and queen of hope
will be coming downstairs soon
in this bed-and-breakfast of the soul
it's table stakes from here on end.

go fetch

fetch me a pail of love.
there's a mighty strong fire of hate blazing
in the hearts of the lost.
i'd throw that pail of love
hoping to aid and abet the healing process.
fetch me humans that can live together.
i walk down the endless hospital corridors
on every gurney lies debris of humans who couldn't hear
each other
i stroll across the fractured moon.
the land is very confused when you put your foot down
on it.
do i run left?
do i hide right?
put me in my rocking chair
i'll be old mose from john ford's great film *the searchers*
he was the guy who survived the comanches
by pretending to be crazy in the head
played wondrously by hank worden.
sitting in my rocking chair on the burning front porch
the majorettes parade by
their body armor a trifle thin.
fetch me something edible.
hunger possesses me.
better than the devil, i guess.
i'll eat the written law.
it's got a lot of fat on it.
fetch me a home of improvisation.
i'd like to enter my house justified
like peckinpah's steve judd in the beautiful *ride the high
country*
beautifully rendered by joel mccrea.
fetch me my santa suit and rent something resembling
reindeer.

they expect me to ho ho ho and i'm not sure where i
left my script.
the earth woke up a few hours ago.
did you sleep okay? i had to ask.
fetch me a vacation and a quiet place to burrow.
the city fathers are looking for empathetic mothers.
king kong and godzilla joined the peace corps.
it's a new day, my friend.
i'll help you tote home those groceries.
just keep my sandwich fresh.
when your back gets up
i got this chiropractor part of me
that can smile if you play the right melody.
the earth asked me for a couple of dollars.
i wrote it a poem.
fetch me no more people who feel they need to fetch.
the new museum just opened.
nobody's yet decided what kind of a museum it'll be.
it feels fun on the soles
wandering its halls.

the eternal struggle

there's a struggle walking cocky down the hall
chest out, muscles making noise
such a struggle is boring and all too obvious
i'd like to strangle it at times
bring it back down to what passes for earth
get over yourself, struggle
everyone's got one
you're not that special
we're lucky to wake up
in some type of seemingly one piece
count all the ways the body can fall apart
don't forget the head, either
i'd love to declare a moratorium on strife, despair, fear,
and angst
but they all keep getting in and out of limos
you can only pull the emergency cord so many times
before the driver kicks you off
there's uncertainty in the cracker jack box
it'll take a lot of dying to meet my deductible
it does me good to see the lovers reaching out for one
another
in the years of blindness
there's a struggle sitting on your face
when you just want to relax and unwind
pressure is writing a series of memoirs
be careful about nicking yourself if you're on blood
thinners
the complacent people are on a long vacation
send condolences if you have the energy
sometimes the struggle tries on your favorite clothes
sometimes the struggle crawls into bed next to you
i'm sick and tired of the demands the struggle makes
i'd like to kick it in the tender spot

every hardass truly has a tender spot
the era of hardasses has dwindled into ash
the vulnerable orchestra has taken center stage
play one of the old bloody songs
the songs that stood their ground
despite all that strife, despair, fear, and angst
still getting in and out of their limos
the planet is a very strange motel room
sometimes the bed does massage your tired bones
sometimes the bed has spikes
you count your blessings
if you don't have any you can count chickens and
sheep
the eternal struggle just raised the rent
our co-pay keeps rising
the lovers still find each other
call it intuition
maybe even some eclectic faith
i feel their empathy
and take a deep breath.

sick ducks on ice

the sick ducks are skating on suspicious ice
all the things that were meant to withstand
suddenly seem frightfully thin.
the amiable men and women suddenly refuse to answer
your phone calls
they never open up when you knock on their doors
there's a new shopping center for the wounded,
maimed, and lost
and the automobile drivers here run you over as you're
in the crosswalk
somebody run out and get a keg
it's time to unwind
baby just began making complete sentences
fuck off, he said in his crib
yes, you can ask me to wash your dishes
but you better help me clean all the blood up first
the sick ducks all wanted a nice vacation
but a lot of motels aren't sick-duck friendly.
once in awhile they might let in a healthy duck
but none of them live in this part of town.
the city fathers have okayed the construction of
a brand-new highway
that will run north and south through my brain
a lot of trees reside there
go on, i dare you, pick an apple and take a bite.
all kinds of people live there
some of them walk on water
some of them live in cardboard boxes
strange countries are seeking recognition
every passing second
the officer who arrested you for impersonating a human
is considered uneven in his total honesty
ambivalent hired killers
are federal justices

writing their names on the bathroom walls
with magic markers
john wayne should have never played genghis khan
all those folks on that shoot getting cancer
the atomic bomb tests in utah, sweetie, they say
late at night in the bowling alleys of remorse
where the pins are good intentions
knock 'em down and win a kewpie doll full of amnesia
sometimes i talk to my sick duck
my sick duck laughs and rolls across the floor
i went to college and hard books fell on my head
they read my arteries and giggled
come morning the flesh-eating zombies
(i remember in the old days when zombies
didn't eat flesh)
will be tap dancing on their way to the big fiesta
mariachi bands in every asylum
the sick ducks are in the unemployment line
the line gets longer every time you inhale
somebody grab me a number
somebody make us whole
we're walking in some heavy-duty dark
can't make out the exit
we'll have to learn to feel one another
no introductions ever needed
you be truly you
i'll try and be me
we'll make it to the movie theater before the feature
begins
all those trailers
don't know if the movie's any damn good
my sick duck had a fine time with it
he quacks quotes from it all day and night
makes it hard to sleep

i woke up with my sick duck squatting on my chest
he thought i was water
our bodies indeed are watery
sometimes our bodies are graves
sometimes our bodies are odd universes
with minds of their ungovernable own
my body would like your body close by
there's gnarly weather ahead
the deck is not steady
we'll need some good music
something strong to drink and smoke
our sick ducks will be healed on TV
all will be forgiven
the bipolar people will settle down easy in the north
and south
our hearts are stories
printed in such tiny print
you'll need a telescope to get the texture
our bodies are rogue planets
in a solar system that has no oversight
my sick duck will become a new senator
my sick duck will cure what ails you
he tells me this and begins to shed feathers
i take the feathers and make a flag
i plant the flag in the heart of the new earth
the gnarly weather tries to rip my flag to shreds
my flag spits in the eye of the gnarly weather.

wounds of love

the thermos is full of an alien life-form
which in perfect pitch
demands i take it to my wound of love
the wound of love has been in county jail for awhile
something about unpaid parking tickets
it sings at night in its holding cell
ballads that turn your heart into the appalachians
hazel dickens runs for high office
the knitters come calling
i vow never to put cultural references in a poem
anymore
then get buried by my dissembling
the wounds of love work out at the gym
they need to get ready for the big grudge match
i saw big grudge and his lame sidekick not-so-big grudge
eating too fast at the KFC
we won't go into mcdonald's ever again, said big grudge
they kill their chickens painfully
why did the chicken cross the road, the chief
of police asked
to find a better mortgage, i said
you win the key to the city, scott
i tried to open it up
the key broke in the lock
oh well
i would of run it into the ground
like george bush
whatever i touch turns to shit
best to wear gloves
leave no trace
the forensic experts are bicycling down from up high
they'll figure who did what to whom
all in the sacred name of those pesky wounds of love
the chickens revolted

pecked ronald mcdonald to death and then some
call the escort service
tell them who you might be
compatible humans with long legs
jammed in tiny cars
riding up and down
on a catatonic saturday night
the last drive-in is showing
the 3-D version of the wounds of love
everyone on the screen is on their game
not sure what the game is
but they're on it
the war came over this morning
do you have any sugar i can borrow?
sorry, don't use it
the war began to sob
you mean i got to drink my coffee black?
we all have to make sacrifices, i said
ripping my heart out and handing it to the war
this will sweeten your coffee
thank you, kind sir
the war limped off, hugging its wounds of love

with one less heart
suddenly i feel much lighter
i begin to float
i rise to the occasion
don't really know what occasion it might be
but i rise to it and nobody will feel any pain.
pain was last seen fleeing the city
in a stolen volkswagen.
destination everywhere
proceed with extreme caution
as pain is extremely contagious.

suicide river

i'm riding the two-dollar all-day florence rhody
express bus
where mike the driver knows everyone by their
first name
you pretty much see the same folks riding
most popular destinations are safeway,
grocery outlet, and
freddie myers
temporarily mike stops at safeway
up ahead i see the regular florence taxi driven by
another mike
who sometimes subs on the rhody express
look, it's the other mike, i say
my mike then tells me the other mike's son is in the
hospital
that at the old age of seventeen or eighteen he tried
to kill himself
the air momentarily gets put on hold
i try to get my head around the image of life being
so unbearable for
somebody so young they'd try to take themselves
out of the game
before the two-minute warning.
just the other night obama in his non–state of the
union speech
which resembled a state of the union speech
said we need to get education up and running
because our future is in the hands of our young
that way too many kids are not even finishing high
school
i dumbly ask if anyone knows why the kid tried it
mike doesn't know
i speculate if the other mike knows why his son
attempted it

sometimes when you break up with the one you feel
should love you
the burden gets so mentally heavy you lose your
backbeat
i knew a great guy full of energy
when a woman rejected his feelings for her
he shot and killed himself
there are so many ways to die
seventeen- and eighteen-year-olds should be strutting
and taking no prisoners
once the life expectancy of man was somewhere in the
forties
now it's somewhere in the seventies and usually beyond
the other mike's son lives despite his intent
will he try it again?
what does this do to the chemistry of the family?
will the merry-go-round ground to a halt?
and its horses all become dog food
i didn't even ask my mike if the kid left a note
since he survived .
was it a suicide attempt meant as a warning
or did he really mean to take the leap and just landed a
few inches
short of the edge
the bus ride began innocent enough
but now as i get off at my stop
i begin to feel a chill
someone else on the bus said
the incidences of teenagers killing themselves are way up
there's something amiss in the drinking water
there are scratches on the CD
if the future is really in our young
they need to get past their teens
there used to be a place in storytelling called
lovers' leap
no black boxes ever found in such wreckage

i look up at my little piece of florence sky
today it's blue and clear
but storm clouds can and do come in from
the sea awful fast
and it can all change its clothes in a few seconds
there must be a long waiting room in heaven
wherever that might be
where suicides sit waiting for their interview
something like the unemployment office
you take a number and when the guard calls it
you tell them just why you had to take your
hand out of the game
certain religions frown on it
others seemingly don't care
teenagers need to roar and tumble
not put themselves in body bags
they can go to war for that
i turn my living-room light on
i remember i'm no teenager anymore
knock on wood, mr. scott
the edge never appealed to me
the dark water never rose that high
if our future
if we really have one
is in our young
they need to be able to take the heat a little better
because the heat is always going to be there
. and then the big freeze
the big heat, the big freeze, they don't often make
allowances for appearance or age
if the other mike's son was standing before me
i'd hug him and tell him please hang on
i don't know what's eating you up
but hopefully it'll get indigestion and spit you out
i guess i'm lucky
it hasn't got that dark in my bloodstream just yet

doesn't mean it might not one day get there
but not now and seemingly never
nothing is ever as it seems
they used to say poets killed themselves a lot
not everyone can be hart crane, anne sexton, sylvia
plath
that room can, at times, be alluring
but you need to keep your wits about you
even if you don't have any
the world will ram its body into you
a metaphysical slamdance
you gotta roll with it
or go under
i hope the other mike's son
can step back a few feet
from that inviting edge
and take a slow deep breath
we're going to need him
to keep us in the dance
we're going to need him
to help show us the way.

lowdown dirty shame

lowdown dirty shame's been talking behind your
steadfast back
saying all sorts of specious shit about your lifestyle
why do you smile and put up with it?
you stand on rickety tables and fall, breaking bones
are you in love with self-punishment?
lowdown dirty shame is writing a cookbook
and you're one of its ingredients
what temperature should i preheat you at?
in the halls of the supposed holy
where you get baptized every morning by bullets
the philosophers are at a loss for words
everything under the sun
even under a few rocks
has been said and retold countless times
lowdown dirty shame is pregnant
it won't reveal the father
maybe it was you
could have been me
we were coming and going all over the place
no time to reflect
no time to hesitate
godzilla went to the mayo clinic
he came out a non-lizard
lowdown dirty shame is about to get sacked
the economy, you probably know
its bank account is dangerously feeble
lowdown dirty shame is used to living in style
three houses
four cars
a debonair wife
two mistresses with names you can't get a handle on
lowdown dirty shame just wrote its will
not liking any of its kids

it cut them all out
it's leaving everything to bigfoot
bigfoot will have to finally show up before congress
he's been given subpoenas over and over
he never shows
a broken record
if he wants that money
he'll have to come on down
pick door number three, monty
lowdown dirty shame claims it drank with kerouac
and ghostwrote bukowski
it's lying
all those years it was hungover in prep school
it wore a uniform that blinded anyone who looked at it
lowdown dirty shame is the new winner on
american idol
what a voice! the judges mutter
i taught the sonofabitch to sing
one day in a shower
that never stopped falling.

politics

not that important

the war hero presidential candidate said the troops
coming home from iraq
were not all that important
casualties are what count
that mind-set explains the vets living on the street
the hospitals here that aren't prepared
in order for you to rate
you need to be dead, apparently
the government even lied badly about those
who came home and committed suicide
i guess the war hero knows what's important and what
isn't
this same war hero didn't sign the GI bill of rights
go war hero, go go go
turn the key hear him sing
i'm your true candidate of change
i'm your daddy warbucks
those soldiers coming home
obviously need some PR people, maybe a lobbyist or
two
i understand iraq, john mccain sang from the corner,
in a very precise tone of voice
feel the pain first, honey
could you open a window please
lots of gagging going on
don't point your gun at me
only silver bullets can bring down the wolfman.

Dead Man's Soiree

Don't mention the rising casualty numbers.
Give us a sweet big kiss, right on the executive
branch lips.
Jesus loves George Bush, who in turn loves you with
arms wide open.
Henny Penny lives in Donald Rumsfeld's vulnerable
heart.
Rudy Giuliani and Hillary Clinton challenge one another
to Donkey Kong.
The Mideast keeps on turning and burning.
The Baathists are taking a shower.
Knock down all the doors,
toss the folks onto the floor,
handcuff them and drag off
the eldest son.
The oldest sun beats unmercifully down
on all the sweating heads of yes.
Rice, Rumsfeld, Wolfowitz,
Cheney, Bush
strays meowing in the dark
listen to their blood,
it is talking angrily and lying with essence.
Santa Claus hung Saddam Hussein
and his reindeers' heart rates have accelerated.
In the marketplace
the starving impresario
does the ambidextrous two-step.
Did the bleeding lovers make their getaway?
Car bombs smile and whisper soft resonance in your
ear.
Grab ahold of the point of no return.
Stand in the corner and sing it like a man.

habeas corpus hoedown

tony scalia and his family the supremos
invite you to a black-tie gala.
tony's got some of his boys in the back
beating the corpus out of habeas.
quick, get the iodine.
the score five to four.
don't let tony do time in gitmo.
john mccain sleeps in sean hannity's tongue.
i know i meant what i thought my advisor told
me to say.
i declare all-out war against the terrorist fist bump.
it's getting hot and rugged in the sandbox.
if you hit obama with your lunchpail
do it when nobody's looking.
congress takes it executively in the ass.
dick cheney as ygor, the faithful servant with the
crooked heart.
john mccain swears he is strong
will change his wrestling name to johnny macabre.
i can bend gitmo detainees with my mind.
clarence thomas, who lives in tony's robes
yells, i can do the fist bump too.
it's open season
everybody raise their rifle.
something calling itself the constitution
thought it had something to say.
tony stares into his mirror
beats his chest.
i am somebody.
i'm a justice.
kiss me in the hard-to-pronounce part of my body.
torture in every kiss.

south of any border

the war decided it was tired and quit
all by itself
it threw its uniform into the river
without it you can't begin to tell it from the rest of
the gang
ali baba keeps counting thirty-nine thieves
somebody went AWOL
he probably went south of any border that would have
him
the men and women there are rumored to be photogenic
the war's in a twelve-step program
each step takes months
the gentle side of man throws a rent party
please stand back ten feet on occasion and let things
grow
the war wants to take your daughter by the hand
the road could use some repair
the men and women condemned to walk it
got a few tricks left
just about eight in the evening
with the air learning to cool down
never demand all that much
get by with what you get
sounds good if you can hoof it
the twelve disciples of incoming
duck your skull gingerly
the war rolled itself up in the map
the gods play hide-and-go-seek
don't let your heart disappear
there was this real good reason for humankind
sort of forgot it
we remember what we are
south of all our borders

the poets that we are
crazy with life
hitch forward
the song, busted, in pain, in need of morphine
plays
the war shot itself in the right big toe
now they gotta send me home.

Obama's Passport File

I was just a bit too curious.
I wanted to see what places Barack Obama traveled to.
I hear traveling is a good thing and I,
the lowly flunky that I am,
never travel anywhere.
Actually I heard Barack was from outer space
and not of our kind.
I just had to see which planet he came from.
I almost went into Hillary Clinton's passport
as I heard she liked to go around the world
but was afraid if I got caught
Bill would strike me dead.
Barack seemed a soft touch compared
to the Clintons.
I didn't mean anything bad.
I did tell Condi that Barack came from Mars.
John McCain should be able to use that.
Most solid Americans don't want Martians in the
White House.
They're just too untrustworthy and probably
would do anything to further their Martian
way of life.
Most Martians are Muslims.
So maybe you can fault me for being curious
but I am a good American and
a solid piece of work.

drink it quick

miss america's varicose veins shed light on our
downtown skin
risky business all around
drink it quick, the president sang
he was off key
a monster lived in his hair
roll them strange dice
karl rove wants my private stash
sad armies sway
the earth lit something up
please breathe deep
my baby knows eight languages
they all say at the end of day
the same thing.

ginseng river

the information almanac makes a good murder weapon
knowledge, in a bit of retroactive bewilderment,
sits in a rocker
alongside ginseng river
the insects are huge
makes a man want to become an acoustic instrument
somebody's in the basement
wailing on a busted piano
don't show any bodies
this is a war with no corpses
on an unsteady end of earth
we pirouette
god's on SSI
beer's on me
your mortgage is safe in ginseng river
don't forget your cue
the new highway drives through our hearts
no time to reset the clock
storm coming.

Ugly Is as Ugly Does

Paul Bremer takes a crash course in learning Arabic.
The monster stirs on the bottom of the ocean floor.
The Iranians shot down their own passenger jet,
they just dressed up as the U.S. Navy.
The monster is photogenic.
I'm a Baathist for your love.
Shia weep for me.
You got the Mesopotamian blues.
Darkness caresses your ability to hear.
The elephant in the room looks dangerously familiar.
Do they still sing Hallelujah in Fallujah?
Infrastructure punctured ear sweet surrender's leer.
Hang them from every tree.
Palestine is relocated to Northern Ireland.
Kiss the Blarney Stone.
Am I truly Black? asks Condosleazy Ice.

gutless love

john conyers wrestles karl rove for the last gun.
dark forces on your pizza
very tasty.
sitting on the earth's subpoena
whistle-blower's lips sewn shut.
rumors of something
even humanity.
the united states of hillary.
dylan said presidents stand naked
but the outgoing clown broke the x-ray machine.
abe lincoln too suspended habeas corpus.
a man without a gut went on TV and said i love you.
sometimes pain only lasts six minutes.
do not demand armless people go bowling.
just a few seconds left on the clock.
your dance card is full but you never learned to come
in out of the rain.

drowning prohibited by law

the lifeguard is a wimp.
he tried to lift the country up.
it snapped his vertebrae.
don't go into that room all by yourself
go in heavily armed.
my shoulder demands to be let in due to rain.
if drowning is truly prohibited by law
why do so many race to the water's edge?
make my future medium-well.
the court jester has appendicitis.
the intersection ahead does not speak english.
okay by me.
gestures and grunts say a lot.
tonight, something edible on the fire.
the band plays "sweet sixteen."
bad boys bore the shit out of me.
the coroner pronounced us man and wife.
follow the money.
oh, there isn't any.
so sorry.
the surgeon general warns
hate can be intoxicating.
turn your weapons in at the door.
i'll be your driver tonight.

my country 'tis of gutless thee

where's that spread they told us would be on the
table, ready for eating
didn't they know it's just another age of uncertainty
humans bump up against other humans who begin to
look
the same
better wear shin protectors
my country's getting out of the hospital soon, i hope
that slobbering dog with the sharp teeth
a rollover for any piece of meat
a new book fell out of the sky
it hurt our heads all at once
the critics ring up a big liquor bill
gets to be that way sometimes
folk heroes might be okay
let me know when you find one
my country swears it wants to watch the comedy network
i guess it might learn something
my baby rolls downhill
when she lands all bets are off

my baby told me privately that god took her to the
movies
i've seen those actors
they work way too hard.

point of no return

specialists sit quietly awaiting your call
they are convinced they know you and can help
all you wanted was a taxi
clean air
places to comfortably fall
few and in between
the heat promises it'll go down one day soon
room service teaches us what to do in case of an
attack
lonesome armies bathing in the light of the moon
the point of no return looks just like more of the
same road
mapmakers wait for their cue
a little grace goes a long way
bigger than life won't fit in the envelope
we got to say their names as they come
mankind a swinging door
go in, go out
break open a barrel
specialists glowing in dark closets
they swear you know yourself
you're beyond help
the point of no return feels a chill
get it something hot
rest awhile.

purgatory yodel

i think this new deck of cards won't lie
everyone claims they're an ace
all i wanted was a good book
and some time to wash my face
the sound of a somewhat busted-down piano
time to stumble uptown
new languages for the asking
purgatory yodel
the campfire girl smiled
when saxophones taught
i think this new way of life
needs a drink
dancing room moon
shake it captain
shake it or lose
this new deck of cards is brought to you
by the powers which be
fire in the hole
go on, say you're sorry
make a big dumb muscle
snow white knew severn men
she told all years later
you glow in radioactive love
which side do you belong to? asked the spoilsport
i'm in every tree
trying to juggle
the rocks aim at your head
you got to dance
dancing's good
it helps you lose weight.

lunch meat of the poor

there's radioactivity in the lunch meat of the poor
a new wonderful thing is coming straight at you
can't begin to wonder how fast a condemned man can run
it's getting hot in very awkward places
the hotel desk clerk gives us a funny look
i got a pogo stick that's kind of sick
it won't let me reach the stars
sleepwalkers seek someone to awaken with
happy meals for the first seventy-five customers
heaven turned itself in to the proper authorities
there's a brand-new golf course
in the lunchboxes of the poor
help me pronounce the people who live there
the devil's got a new friend
their eyes dive into each other
here come the seven dwarves
snow white felt this weight
she really intends to shimmy
on the corner
of apoplexy and divine
here comes the weight they warned us about
i got a spare key
there's a new way of bobbing and weaving
in the lunch meat of the poor
the last bus is about to head out
bring your severed relations
to the midnight show.

hoedown

snarling right-wing talk radio types turn into flour
as the main act for tonight
attempts to carry any tune that will have him
i hear the progress reports will be falling from the
sky any minute
i read your book, can i get a part in the movie?
tonight is the blood transfusion
you can get in cheap
the opening act is wary
despite it all, hoedown
the ice cracks
drink up
mountains wake up
follow the river
as the main act for tonight
is us
murder in the air challenged hoedown
two out of three
i wish i could sing all night long
but my voice would run off
there it hops right now
and the main act tonight
is everyone.

refreshing bakery of the heart

all cemeteries will simply vanish
the president said to a tree
it was the end of the final act
but the actors are confused
somebody switched plays
not what we meant
not what was written
raise your hands
ward off the blow that's sneering at you
new oceans are thirsty
newer days are slowly crawling
give it time
said the last bus out of town
in the refreshing bakery of the heart
men and women eat too much and explode
give it all you got
said the guy at the wheel
nobody knows where we're running
i will find you when the lights die
i will be in every room.

for the life of me

hillary clinton sells me poetry books
underlined in red
my dog friedrich dug up a miniature civilization
they made him take it back
the master of all ceremony
lives in a bunker
i'd like to get any recipe
that won't burn
john mccain told my bathtub an off-color joke
act one went on all night
for the life of me
you could hear them sing
the dancers swear there's time
all rivers need a sea
call me when the war ends
grab a towel 'cause you'll sweat
the room just gets bigger.

ways and means

ways and means got popped for indecency
come and teach me to read
pumpkin done went splat
get the cleanup crew
the evening news just shot itself
will you make the wake?
senators crawling through air ducts
claim the playground is made up of natural
old men and women will canoe you across
the big belligerent muddy
you won't pay too much
just expose your ways and means
the lifeguard is inattentive
the water never was that deep
come and teach me the bone
who lives there
how the doors open when you smile
the war is not going anytime soon.

you bet your ass

stories stand on the corner
you might not like some of the outcomes
then again the music
the fragile last hand of man
one bony motherfuck
holding up a rhythm section that will not die quietly
coming or going
just about daybreak
you bet your ass
and then some
the waitress will tell us about the special
jukebox empathy
man's coming up to bat
i just got to make the weekend sale
stories in every corner
blood patiently at the door.

safe harbor

in just a few seconds we'll reach safety
all we got to do is never lie again
sometimes the truth just doesn't want to live
we'll find a reason to get together and push the rock
uphill
there's a safe harbor hanging from your belt
the supreme court will sit on us, hold us down
mr. reckoning just checked into his suite
prepare for battle stations
if chills apply, step closer to the fire
heartache and heartbreak
how big is the territory?
do you have a darling?
can your darling dance?
if you don't know the right moves
they easily discuss chopping off your legs
sometimes it's what people think they die for
sometimes just a passing fancy
land seems nearer
soon, sleep
it's almost the end of the final quarter
you need them for the washing machine
i lost my nerve in the spin cycle
the posse rode so hard their horses went on strike
it's the third door down the hall on the right
nobody really knows the end of the story
a tropical island would be very good
nobody remembers swimming
for years the janitor sweeps
he'd be the one to ask.

hanging in there

fresh blood wallpaper
hate rides a large trail
must have been humans once
how we talked about love
did it still exist?
did everyone want to outlive their best intentions?
dark amusement park
waiting on us at end of day
i've been on all those rides
and even if i didn't
they still grab for you
in the cold safety net
we flounder remarkably
who wrote this goddamn chapter?
how many pages more
the light fades
it's okay, the liar smiles
you can read the rest in the dark
hate yawns, stretches
humans once lived somewhere
maybe even here
hanging in there, the ceiling read
that's who and what we were
hanging in there
i shake the wounded music box
i recall a backbeat
that was big enough for all of us
but those hours got scattered
in some dumb-ass wind
i still shake my music box
enemy aircraft rolling in off the tongue
oh well

god said he understood men and women
he lied
he meant well
the posse is never coming home
but their horses
sure dance good.

traffic jam

i know what democracy is, the chimp swore.
gods for hire.
a vision in the outhouse
worrying about which profile
to give the camera.
late at night when the pain drinks itself asleep
they ask you to speak precise english.
government of the people by the people for the people.
people are strange, sang streisand
in the body of jim morrison
as the much-anticipated x-rays
got snarled in a traffic jam.
i know what freedom said.
you won't like the tone.
a house so close
you could be a brick in it.
a rest stop so far
it'll be years before you get heard.
let the youngsters kill and be killed back.
the old rocking chairs crack
the winning lotto ticket on fire.

Phone Call at 3 A.M.

My phone rings at 3 in the morning
and it's Hillary Clinton telling me she's on the way
over
to commander-in-chief me.
I think you got the wrong guy,
says tired old me,
the last time somebody dared
commander-in-chief me I wound
up doing penance in an eerie hospital.
John McCain and I arm wrestle every day
and sometimes he lets me win.
God loves a true winner, I mumble,
and fools stand on every corner
beating their breasts in inane ferocity.
I will purr in your ear, Mr. Wannberg,
says the ex–First Lady,
you will light up and be reborn.
Make my lungs happy and my foot metaphysical if you
intend to press my everloving buzzer, sweetheart.
It's three fucking A.M.,
get some damn sleep.
She gives up on me and slams the phone down.
I shut my eyes and the electoral college
explodes into little pieces of skin and bone.
From day one I come running
singing those sleep-deprived nights of sometime love.

undone

ann coulter leaps nude out of my high-fiber cereal
oozing i love joe mccarthy warbles.
nowhere on the box is any warning.
i turn on my TV and the bleeding claws of dick cheney
reach out to grab me.
hillary clinton hides in my closet
declaiming she knows better now than then.
what is a poor soul to do?
dog calls collect
and demands i still consider him my best friend.
the full moon is getting out of jail
which means the wolf in us all will be over shortly.
rush limbaugh puts his cigar out in the dim-witted face
of john mccain.
lovers attempt to climb insurmountable mountains.
the doctor says dancing is still very mortal.
the deaf and the blind will be our designated drivers.
mediocre men and women inflate with some new gas
that has the arbiters of taste walking backward and
scratching their asses.
there are incandescent morons at loose in the
machinery.
the years fingernail our sense of fair play.
time to embrace the everloving chaos.
time to be undone.
bill o'reilly sticks his head out of my toilet.
i'd call a plumber but they won't cross the striking
writers' picket line.

mañana american eagle

for dave alvin, the man

the retreating army marching along my tongue
put some spice into the body politic
children in high places
big men collapse
paradise committed to a sanitarium
one day soon your own personal moon
octane burns a hole right through
sweet sixteen with scars to match
mañana american eagle
seasoning a bit oversweet
hold on to your day job
the dance card is late
big guys broken by tiny rocks
almost home
across those unknown rumors of sea
here comes the slow tune
i can handle that
did you see how fast the race was run?
the brand-new sand
in just one more old box
go on, pick up your instrument
it's going to need you.

out west, somewhere

i'm riding with a posse that keeps falling off their
horses
blame it, no doubt, on the weather
houdini will now break out of the president's ability
to supposedly think
out west, somewhere, the hands of surgeons
law enforcement officials implode
she takes it all off
books are written
turned into inept film versions
the guy hired as shotgun guard in collusion with the
outlaw gang
my country has a bad toothache
he's very fearful of dentists
don't drink just any water
some of this love might be poisoned
my country is having a baby
nobody knows the father
out west somewhere
sleeping peaceful with coyotes.

negligent

dark forces congregate
bring the family all the beer you can
negligent rooms at affordable prices
fools on parade
their tongues are ten miles wide
if i had known better
do it all again
the confused medicine of our lives
sway now
the king and queen of nothing much
will be in attendance
jokes somersault from the sky.

state of something union

Iraq is love
says Jorge the decider
and my devil's glass Johnson
speaks directly to God.
The ducks may be bleedng
but the pond's water will soothe your burning soul.
My rear end never has to do time on the firing line
and my ability to mangle language
never wanes.
Kiss my everloving royal ass
while the Earth checks into rehab
and quietly dies a little more each day.

late at night

my TV is tired of staring back at me
the mousketeers land on the dark end of the street
they got democracy in the late-at-night bag
the world is waiting on the new gold bathrooms
jesus christ from now on will be neon
the president drinks truth syrup
it tries not to let him lie so much
a terrorist hid in the president's hair
the hours are finishing their shifts
soon all of us will be home
one of us might find a schedule of events
sometimes it's nothing but a series of avalanches
the trains claim they run on time
late at night a few of us die
there's music in every room
the only ticket needed
one's flesh.

appeasement blues

a rifle in every box of cereal
even instructions on how to use it
somebody's squinting over our shoulders
the doctor vows he's got our back
that leaves a lot to be desired in the front
the young pistoleros all suffer from back injuries
the appeasement blues is buying everyone a round
make room for me in the corner
where the traffic at times is bearable
katrina wants to apologize to new orleans
she's anybody's woman now
george bush has "stay the course" welded to his forehead
neville chamberlain's umbrella full of holes
our canoe is beginning to sink
nobody really knows how deep we can go
the chief executioner is afraid of mice
pile wounds in the to-do tray
everybody gets married on the same day
bring the wild turkey
we'll take notes
which of you are truly fit? asks the game show host
the border drowns
they're letting us out on our own recognizance
i'm going to disneyland.

rap to 2009

wouldn't it be a really happy new year
if all the folks who got laid off in 2008
suddenly had jobs on january 1.
perhaps all those mortgages blowing in the changing wind
would stop, comb their hair, and smile.
i walk around in squares
because all the circles were missing in action.
ring around the rosie
used to be a popular expression here.
universal health care
starring boris karloff and bela lugosi
those undisputed horror kings of universal.
the new president
you know, the muslim terrorist,
he saddles his horse january 20.
israel and hamas gouge each other in gaza
to usher in this new year.
violence in afghanistan is way up.
george bush is telling one and all
that the last eight years have been profoundly moving.
the new year is sort of the old year in many ways.
it stares at itself in the magic mirror
am i getting a year older? is my hair on fire?
father time and mother space
sit in rocking chairs smoking poor people
rolled up in seventy-billion-dollar-bailout rolling paper.
i talk to my dinner
my dinner does not reply.
in 2009 honesty claims it's the best policy.
if i could only find some
we'd test that statement.
love will be legal in 2009 i hear. all those lovers in jail
will be pardoned.
george bush pardons himself.

i beg your . . .
i snarl at my dinner
answer me, damn you, or i'll eat you.
in 2009 people will need less food.
promotions will be whispered.
rush limbaugh will steal barbra streisand from james
brolin.
the supreme court will rule against itself and close up
shop.
courtney love will kill rambo.
jehovah will deny he ever was a witness.
it's all hearsay, honey.
my heart will still be in the game.
sometimes the load seems beyond endurance.
sometimes the weight threatens to crack me in half.
hell, i'm half-baked anyway.
i go left when i assuredly mean right.
my hometown is wherever i am.
my eyes need adjusting.
turn some lights on if you please.
the new year crawls across no-man's-land
it has a new song in its blood.
we need to listen
we need to see.
i open my eyes every time simon says "open."
no, not paul simon.
father time throws mother space onto the bearskin rug.
it's time for family hour.
i hope our new president can get something done.
the abominable snowmen are having an important
jam session in the himalayas.
i stand on my head
the blood rushes something fierce.
2009 grabs my face.
it stares through me.

i begin to tell it this new poem.
it begins
wouldn't it be a really happy new year.
don't you dare say any more, 2009 grumbles.
i just got born.
i need some space.
i need to figure a plan.
okay, i sigh.
i'll turn my clock back.
when you feel you're ready
you'll know where i can be found.
2009 nods, mumbles, dives through my window.
it's not that far down to the ground.
only about a year.
happy new year, my TV says to my stereo.
technology can be so warm.

michele bachmann blues rag

chris matthews set me up
he forced me to say what i did.
i take it back.
forget my demanding the media investigate congress's
unamerican democrats
those were my double's words.
i was inexplicably possessed.
please RNC put money back into my reelection campaign.
my name is much easier to say, much more so than my
opponent's.
i don't get my words out right sometimes
i guess they're not really my words.
i'm channeling an ancient goddess warrior.
i love my minnesota
my minnesota loves me.
so what if the democrats are traitors
even they have wives and kids.
don't really put their evil ways under a microscope.
live and let live.
i get it now.
i'm just doing the right thing.
chris matthews wanted me to take a hard fall.
i'm just a poor confused soul-searching republican.
can i sing now?
can i baby-sit your children?
i truly do love you.
let me prove myself.
turn the lights down low.
put your most relaxing music on.
i will show you i'm worthy.
i will atone.

traces of human

the autopsy on the future of the planet
will begin as soon as you take care of the collection
agency
my cyst used to be a CEO
not sure what it does to make ends meet these days
and what if the ends never meet?
will their hearts break?
i met somebody one day
i can't claim it was particularly easy
you smile when you feel like screaming
you nod your head as they utter noise
when all you feel like doing is putting tape over their
mouths
some days you meet lots of people
but your ends still come home with you
how about we take a good look at the beginnings?
do the beginnings justify the means?
on mother's day norman bates buys himself a present
he wraps it up very nice
i guess he bakes his own apple pie
norman, you recall, is an avid taxidermist
he stuffed the endangered american eagle
he dressed it up in the american flag
or maybe it was the state flag of ohio
you know, the potentate of barama flag with the big O
the right-wing guy warned us about yesterday
poor ohio, being mistook by right-wing town criers for a
partisan flag
norman mailed his stuffed eagle to would-be vice-
president palin
palin empathizes with children with special needs
and norman certainly qualifies
palin was so impressed she takes the eagle wherever she
goes

she rubs it endearingly when she works the crowd
she just might give it to the secessionist bunch she
and todd hang around with
the same bunch that said damn america
there are terrorists in every woodwind
but the orchestra goes on
best get inside before the rain comes
it's going to be around for days
last night i saw america at the gym
it was kind of wobbly
it's getting up there in age
it's still, however, in the game
keep pumping it
keep attempting to touch your toes
pass that sobriety test, baby
we got places we need to get
you're going to need that license

underdeveloped utopia hoedown

utopia's getting released from the county farm this
morning.
it was arrested for vagrancy and sassed the judge.
that utopia's one stubborn rowdy outlaw.
it walks main street with bowlegs.
utopia needs a cup of strong black coffee.
utopia needs somebody to talk to, to share actual ideas
with.
thomas more wrote on my back, utopia tells a
convenience store owner.
thomas more got his head cut off, the owner replies
drolly.
he died for principle.
was the sun hot when the axe fell?
let the stupid king divorce and remarry.
the stupid kings usually step all over utopia.
the stupid kings have divine right on their scalp belts.
god talks directly to them.
the current stupid king is packing his lunch
and heading down to dallas.
utopia takes a long cold shower.
i got to wake up after these eight years.
morons line up in the cold.
they wave good-bye to the exiting stupid king.
the hospitals are discharging all terminally ill patients.
they need the beds.
utopia will heal them
in the rising floodwater.
i'm looking for a bar stool that will appreciate my fat ass.
i intend to toast utopia a couple of long rounds.
utopia really is a figment of the imagination.
it never existed.
okay by me.
i value the imagination.

it opens a lot of doors and windows for me.
i might not be able to fit through them
but at least they're open.
yesterday two jehovah's witnesses, on foot,
disturbed my reading john d. macdonald's *a tan and
sandy silence.*
we'd like to talk to you about god, they said.
can't god talk about him or her self? does he or she
require front men and women
to explain his or her actions or lack of action?
people blame god for their troubles, they said.
i thought about travis mcgee and really wanted to go
back to my book.
it was another blue-sky day of beauty in florence
after months of windy rain
and here i was trying to take in the blue.
yes, i suppose people do, i said.
they told me god was above being blamed for any
bad stuff that went on in the world.
i could have argued that if god truly created it all
then the bad as well as the good would have to be
assessed.

who invented palestine and israel.
oh, the british invented palestine and the UN created
israel.
who invented the british?
thomas more was british.
his stupid king was british.
who invented them?
god lives in utopia. utopia has a hernia.
utopia has a bladder infection
and a painful swollen scrotum.
the folks gave me a copy of their magazine and walked
away.
i went back to travis mcgee.
john d. macdonald invented him.

utopia claims it's going to write a memoir.
it could be ugly in its beauty.
utopia would like to buy a condo
but is low on funds.
utopia just got laid off.
i hope obama can get utopia a job.
it's a new day, they say.
rejoice and make merry.
thcy toast marshmallows over the fire.
the dragon temporarily seems slain.
the heroes stand humble in the heat.
utopia needs to get laid.
i think it's eyeballing your favorite daughter.

hope in a bottle

they got a sale on hope in a bottle
two six-packs for under ten dollars
you can't go too far
without some hope making noise in your cup
i was walking on this nameless road
it seemed to stretch on for hours
i didn't have to be anywhere or see anyone
i put my feet down and kept walking in something
resembling a direction
i'm pretty shitty when it comes to directions
i know enough not to stand in front of cars
i had a backpack on full of bottles of hope
every now and then i'd open up one
take a long drink and dodge incoming ammo
i think today we might finally win the war
i don't know which war
there are so many of them going on simultaneously
they are killing each other over warehouses full of bottles
of hope
won't you come running when my flashlight breaks
won't you offer shelter when it rains
bring your own sixer of hope
we'll drink it down all through the night
won't you help me pick up the dead
help me get them interred
i think the war finally won us
it wasn't easy
it looked into our respective eyes
i know you all, it said
when the war talks this smooth
all you can do is swear, i believe
even jesus sometimes had shit stains in his underwear
everybody wants to drive a hard bargain
everyone wants to reach the top of the mountain

i hear the war is lonely
it'd like to drink a bottle of hope
i rode the merry-go-round
the horses all laughed
all the first ladies walk the streets after curfew
monsters in the gas tank
i rub some hope on your aching muscles
i'm swinging from tree to tree with my friends
the monkeys
it's good exercise
builds tone
tell me when we reach the next rest stop
tell me when we cross the imaginary border
the fire inside rises
feel the heat and get out of the way
won't you come singing when my ears freeze and fall off
won't you come knocking when my door explodes
i got one bottle of hope left
it's one of those bottles that never gets empty
the war has a migraine
quick, dim the lights
lay me down, let me take my rest
my feet are swollen and my head is shrunk
i don't really care as long as you're around
tap dancing on barbed wire
i love the way you move
i love the way you fly
meet me at the corner of jurisprudence and possible
we'll drink some hope
we'll get rip-roaring mad with hope
when they finally decide to come for us
they won't be able to tell us apart
and what a party that truly will be.

slums of gold

the slums of gold
are having open houses for all the affable
CEOs and financial wizards
who have taken their bailout money
to build shiny brand-new executive bathrooms
and finance relaxing weekend retreats far from
the noise and fear
of the street.
the slums of gold have king-size beds that will
make the most tired and achy
executive feel so human and tender.
special guarded elevators will take these new stylish tenants
to the penthouse, but wait a second,
sometimes the penthouse has no roof
and the vultures soar overhead awaiting their next happy meal.
the slums of gold find themselves eventually
under a fierce rain
which washes that fake gold off
revealing corroded iron and brokedown wood.
it's a new year.
homicide will soon reach its deductible
and its bills will reduce greatly.
the slums of gold are having a block party.
bring all your favorite yes-men and -women, executives.
bring your bylaws and meeting minutes.
you'll have to budget the air
inhale just so much oxygen.
the banks glow in the dark.
they begin to pull up stakes
and slither across the earth
looking for food.

meanwhile, all humans with no health care
whatsoever
become kings and queens for one day.
they are asked to pose for high-profile pictures.
as soon as you're through coughing up blood
could you smile and say cheese?
the CEOs have blood in their underwear.
should they panic?
should they take a happy pill?
all the happy pills forgot their distemper shots.
they are not agreeable this morning.
when you go to open them up to ingest one
they bite your fingers.

bush legacy tour hallucination raga

i gave you eight years of beauty and love
i made the earth fertile and imaginative
i will go down in history as the king of all deciders
i slept with the constitution and it never snored and
woke me up
i never made a mistake i couldn't live with
there's a never-ending price somewhere in this hall of
mirrors
it demands an accounting
i shake myself and blubber
the decider has made his last great decision
distorted, disturbed, disenfranchised, discombobulated
i am mr. clean
i am super-president
i saved america from evil
idiot, my dog sparky drools
there's years of videotape and documentation
even a dumb dog like me can sniff through the record if
he feels like it
go sparky, go, i say

the bush legacy tour can't pull one over your eyes
i put some of the bush legacy tour in sparky's bowl.
he takes a bite, gags, spits it out
are you trying to poison me, scott?
sorry, sparky, i just had to make sure
don't ever second-guess my canine intuition again or
i just might leave and join the circus
now get me some real good dog food and rub my belly
bill clinton messed up the economy, george says with a
smile
sparky raises a leg and unwinds.

the day after

moving day at the big white house
it's finally done.
the decider and his cowgirl are off in texas drinking with
pecos bill.
the new president and his missus partied the night away.
now the work begins.
moving the huge boulder up the hill.
for eight years that boulder has gotten monstrous huge.
poor dick cheney
always lift boxes with your legs, not your back.
seeing him wheeled out reminded me of dr. strangelove.
controversial rick warren talked about us all as one.
will he now go see the film *milk*?
it won't be easy.
a momentary scare at lunch with senator kennedy
getting ill.
he's better today.
that cold cold D.C. weather.
they told william henry harrison to dress warm and keep
his speech short. he did neither
and pneumonia aced him out within three months,
one of the shortest presidential terms in history.
the so-called ranch in crawford needs a new tenant.
the ranch where no livestock lived or produce grew
a ranch in myth only.
the decider is not a cowboy.
ramblin' jack elliott is more of one
and he's the son of a doctor from brooklyn.
people reinventing themselves every day of the week.
the new president speaks complete sentences and can
form thoughts.
the road is long and hard and there will be casualties.
there are always casualties.
it's the process.

with every lotto ticket purchase comes affordable
health insurance.
the world and the united states are dating again.
tentative first kisses.
the hard work is here now and ongoing.
my fingers are crossed.
my heart is open.
the game has changed.
some oxygen is finally, after eight years of strangulation,
getting through.
we take this new ride together.
the streets at times might be uncoordinated.
hang onto the wheel.
buckle up.
sing loud and pay attention.
so many people sleepwalked through the last eight years.
so many people became zombies.
time now to stretch.
put those eight years of bloody sheets
in the washer.
open the damn window.
let some light in.
there are mountains of pain and hurt
that need scaling.
it's going to take time.
some of us have very very little of that.
my fingers are crossed.
my eyes are open.
sometimes the dust gets in.
not a happy thing.
i wipe the dust from my eyes and walk a few inches farther.
it's a new rhythm.
you can get up now and dance.
i know your legs hurt
but give it a try.
sometimes the doctors do care.

frankenstein meets rod blagojevich

bring the family
fun to be had by all
frankenstein impeaches his monster
rush limbaugh chokes on his cigar
governor rod blagojevich swears they're out to get him
george bush, dick cheney, and donald rumsfeld become
new tenants in gitmo
health care for every millionaire
you got to be in the network
if you're gonna get a chance to dance
the dark streets of man
need repaving
obama talks to muslims
jimmy hoffa rises from wherever he's been buried
my time is at hand
i take my bullet-ridden lunchpail
recess is over
i'm on my way to the next big opportunity
turd blossom aka karl rove now has a new subpoena
please don't make me go before congress, mr. obama,
he cries
bring the wife, the mistress as well
all ages welcome
if you can't meet the cover
discuss our sliding scale for the indigent and insane
they just discovered a new planet
called arrogance
citibank lives there
and their special toys that fly in the sky
i'm on my way to the next big prison
the one that offers the best deals
bring the parole officer
bring your head doctor
bill o'reilly's ego explodes and the street-cleaners have a

hell of a time
cleaning up
they haven't discovered the bottom of the well yet
superman took ann coulter home
she turned into kryptonite
it gets a bit confusing in the marketplace
everyone wants the last box of hope
they fight and kick each other for the privilege
the surf's up and it's bloody
bring your body armor
bring your rosary
the new age has just fallen out of its hospital bed
it hit the floor something fierce
quick, run and get a fifth of wild turkey
frankenstein's monster and governor rod
discuss those paranoid villagers with their torches
smoke good, fire bad, says the monster
health care for the elderly, says governor rod
their hearts spark in the incognito night
it makes me proud to be a human
i run into sisyphus on the street
those boulders keep getting bigger every day, he winces
i give him some valium
bring the future
bring your best attitude
the party's just getting good
it's ladies' choice
a mountain grows in the middle of the living room
we'll climb it in tandem
governor rod and frankenstein's monster
go skinny-dipping in the sea of tranquility.

bobby in the box

put a coin in bobby in the box
his head will leap out right at you
katrina was caused by the government messing in your
private moment
tax cuts for the dead and rotting
bobby held his obama voodoo doll up in the light
i'm gonna stick him now with my street knife
poor poor bobby
send him to night school
where the young girls will croon and sway
when he smiles and combs his hair
hot times in the bayou tonight
every man a king, huey said
melt down your gold throne
pour it over wall street's toupee
the carnival is getting ready to leave
count your fingers and change
bobby in the box comes in many flavors
all of them cause ulcers
hang on baby
bette davis said it very clear in *all about eve*
it's going to be a bumpy night.

evidence kit full of anything you need to get by

prove it, my TV screen belched
can humanity ever come to grips with itself?
there is a large cave in the spirit
a lot of people might be hiding in it
some names have been changed to protect the guilty
restitution needs restoration
an evidence kit full of anything you need to get by
falls on my head as i prepare my citizenship papers
the neighborhood animals are up to something
they huddle in the dark
review their respective situations
i tried to review my situation once
but my editor refused my copy
claiming i lacked singular vision and clarity
singular vision, i once read in a controversial history book,
led a pack of infamous outlaws
they sacked the city of i-hope-you-truly-mean-what-you-
say
the detectives investigating my wallpaper
for signs a civilization once attempted to exist here
grow ornery and argue about the 100 best films ever
made
i've seen all 100, i tell them
it was just the same story though
norman bates buried jimmy hoffa in the swamp
shangri-la became chinatown
forget it dog, it's just the pound
risk it, my laptop snarled
can humanity ever safefully slide into home plate?
methuselah does wind sprints
as choreography makes a major comeback
in the lives of double-parked men and women
where did the mayan people go?

here today, most assuredly gone tomorrow
charlie parker, not fess, was the real daniel boone
navigating uncharted depths
the cartographers get together
draw sinister maps on my back
X marks something
the beginning of another story that never ends
every time the storyteller almost gets to the finish line
his or her heart breaks
the paramedics race over with their reindeer
shove it, my telephone coughs
death has call waiting
If you'd like to endure
press the pound key.

the mean streets of love

hurry up and get a good place in line
the mean streets of love are getting a makeover
infrastructure will grow out of your aching back
and the night light will never burn out.
the city fathers and the county mothers
invite you to the wedding of skin and blood.
take the year off from work
you'll easily be covered, or replaced.
reconstruction rears its misshapen face
in the one-way mirror of time.
one cartridge left in the smoking gun
don't use it unless it's act three.
final curtains take their bow
and the mobs give themselves standing ovations.
the mean streets of love
crisscross today's lunch special.
you empty your pockets in front of the judge
he is not impressed with the way you've aged.
sentence: six years of hard human.
it takes so long to walk down the hall
you could have read *moby dick* cover to cover.
shampoo the shrapnel out of your hair.
the new economy condos on the mean streets of love
are so overpriced no one's able to buy.
by the time my front door stumbled into me
afghanistan and iraq had joined bobby jindal at disney
world.
there are hieroglyphics in the carpet.
i can't translate too much for you right now.
my eyes are in denial.
the mean streets of love had heart surgery
early this morning.
crows cawed and rifles recoiled.

all the specialists go mad just about one o'clock.
something in the deep water.
something in the sacred text.
street-sweepers and kings
share the same bathroom.
if you tip the plumbing enough
it'll work.

jubilee

obama wears 666, a scared man tells the camera in the
documentary
right america,
an HBO exploration of the recent campaign by
alexandra pelosi.
he's the devil, and america should be afraid.
i remember the night god and the devil came over to my
apartment on a whim.
whims actually can do you in.
both the devil and god were angry that i hadn't made a
hard-liquor run.
hell, i explained, this town only has one state-run hard-
liquor store and
it's too far for me to walk. go get your own hoodoo.
don't sass back, grumbled god, checking out my DVDs.
sass him all you can, the devil giggled
but i accidentally stepped on his tail and he shrieked.
sorry, i said, but don't get under my feet. they're the only
pair i have.
i see, god said, that you stock no televangelists in your
collection.
well, i answered, i can't understand them most of the
time and my remote's volume control
has been acting suspicious lately.
ted haggard is a good boy, the devil said, nudging god in
the right elbow.
quit milking it, luce, god snarled. it's getting old.
put some rock music on, i wanna dance, the devil
hummed. i remember
the good-old days when rock and roll was called my
music.
he's putting you on, god chuckled. luce is into abba.
well, they do have a following, the devil nodded.
we heard you were having a jubilee, scott, god sighed.

i've always been into a good jubilee. it can make the day
a better prescription
for what hurts your heart. is your heart hurting?
anyone half-assed alive that feels anything resembling
empathy for
humanity can only, at certain times, feel their heart hurt.
i assumed both of them knew that.
the question was rhetorical.
rhetorical questions turn into dust.
my heart's hanging in there, i finally said.
when is the jubilee coming, scott? god asked in a tired
tone.
does jubilee have a younger sister? winked the devil.
jubilee's on a greyhound bus. it could take months.
god and the devil raided my icebox.
there wasn't all that much living there.
for the road, they chirped in unison. i watched them walk
up to highway 101.
god actually was limping a little.
the devil had a bounce to him.
they began shoving my food into their mouths.
visiting your earth can get you hungry, i guess.
they seemed a very odd couple.
but they also seemed in love.
love is hard enough to find in this crazy golf course.
you think you know the terrain of the green you're
playing
but mountains suddenly rise up and block your intended
hole.
when you find it
no matter its configuration
let it be
let it grow
enjoy its energy.

don't legislate its appearance
don't break it apart for not speaking the state language.
the recent campaign, now barefoot and covered in
grime,
hitches a ride in jubilee's faltering greyhound.
when the devil and god came over that night
they didn't wear american flag pins in their lapels.
jubilee called on her cell phone
don't give up, i'm still on my way.
keep the window slightly open
the night air will sing to you.
the ultimate terrorist is irrational fear.
jubilee told me she'd get off at the state-run hard-liquor
store.
bring some wild turkey i tell her.
i look out my window and watch the hordes devour
themselves.
when they stop feeding
they'll need some pepto-bismol.
god and the devil stop at a gas station.
it's oregon
and they get roughed up for trying to self-serve.

recovery

traveling

accidents happen
in the cool light of evening
men and women cry
keep your head down
we hear good things are in the offering
somewhere there is water
cold and thirst quenching
the earth shakes a little
when it goes to pick things up
the village idiots are well dressed
and all ages are admitted
traveling
continents bump up against each other
still time for one last bet
in the house of rock and roll
there is no curfew
i got civilization in my shoe.

that old burning sensation

the world checked into the emergency room
had some kind of fever
broke out in purple spots
everybody claims they want the world to get better
but we're talking HMOs here
the hallway to world's private room
longer each day
somebody lay a comfortable carpet
somebody grab the helm
specialists probed the world
x-rays got took
that old burning sensation
line 'em up to the right, line 'em up to the left
the world took a look in the mirror
it wants to go home soon
sometimes the world forgets its address
you got to take pictures
it'll recognize its house
we'll all meet there
some party.

the house love built

they're coming to pick up the wounded today
they promise there'll be good times coming
everybody will get a shot
i'd settle for some wild turkey
the magician hired to entertain us
looks weirdly familiar
we might have done time together
it's good to have a vocational skill
some people can't help but smash things
i wish they'd take a long vacation
the house love built
is getting worn down
no bother
i can fake sleep anywhere
come, quick with the plasma
tell the honor guard to sit down
whimsy raises its hurting head
asks for our résumé
they're coming to praise one another
in a language that will bury you
everybody will become one
the house love built
perhaps floating on quicksand
asks us to set sail
we are children learning to walk
sometimes we round third base.

the road to recovery

it's all over but the shouting
the phones broke
wounded dollars fall from slippery hands
jesus is getting a makeover
his daddy's got a hangover
i'll scratch your back if you do mine
put the dark into a test tube
call for a pizza
the road to recovery is closed temporarily
for repairs
this hard-to-read book
almost done
bring your RSVP
all night isn't what it used to be
i live in the middle of the water
moving soon to the zoo
the road to recovery
is writing a tell-all memoir
first edition first printing
in the corner of a brand-new basement
lurks love
send a telegram
smoke signals too
today the human race
tomorrow the world.

there was this time

do you remember when jack nicholson didn't overact?
it might even have been summer
everyone went to the beach
don't know who's due first
the huge sea monster or the enemy fleet
the killers grow young and are too sure of their aim
there are some rude things still not itemized
even awakenings
somebody swears they'll pat us on the back
there once was this time
it had trouble sleeping now and then
even the wolfman knows in his heart that the full moon
has to go away
the surgeon's en route
he's got a colorful rep
when your baby comes home radioactive
will you still want to play the game?
when your baby gives you the leprosy
not too much left to say.

there is a radiance

the all-know-it people rant at me in tongues.
since i don't know anything
i promise to join their club.
a radiance once got its mail here
now the window has a hard time opening.
the president rode a donkey
back when parades counted.
a city once lied about its age here
whether too young or too old
no one will claim they can say.
radiance climbed up a dying tree
saw what he wasn't supposed to.
they got gold menus full of food that moves.
soon the headline act will waltz onto stage
and the audience's wounds will stand up and fly away.

they're burning down the dance hall

it simply won't do
sleepwalkers suffering insomnia
the maid service here could be better
some folk heroes have hard right hands
others get lost in the crowd
hell lives around here somewhere
the underage show kicks off at noon
the king and queen are actually talking
pick-up sticks on the river styx
charon plays bo diddley
how tall is man?
can he blot out the sun?
depends on your mood
all the bandits in the world
patiently waiting in ambush
for the only gold shipment
they're about to burn down the dance hall
the healers are a bit green
tell god to bring inhalers
i hear a fiddle in the dark
it's asking my bones to say yes.
i begin to bounce.

everybody

everybody wanted to save you from drowning
you're that well liked
tonight the drinks are on me
the pretty people are doing KP
smoke 'em if you got 'em
blow some of that history to me
median age sweet sixteen
i'll hold up my end of the bar
i'd like to make the bargain mat
softly if you please
everybody knew your name
the guards grow restless
experts will carry the load.

earth shall come knocking

who's on point tonight?
no telling what language is being thrown at you
soon there won't be any more attacks
soon the magician will pull us out of his hat
earth shall come knocking
somebody might be home
in the dropping of temperature
in the house of all trades
the doctors ride skateboards
there are so many keys
i can't figure the one that unlocks the front
we can slip in through the back
nobody will know the difference.

hurt city

timid people still live here
they just changed their names
warriors full of ridiculous noise
assure us they own everything
hurt city demanding a hearing
in some progressive motel room
i'm in steerage with the other freaks
slowly counting sheep
did you see the old lady take it to the mob?
some of us teeter, others totter
free drinks from the well
hurt city in the ER
all we got left are band-aids
who's running this airline?
lots of so-called food on the table
the hungry people got this eerie feeling
upstairs the floor show
timid people your escort for tonight
what name would you like?
hurt city on a late-night talk show
scars and improv
the earth begins to floor the engine.

rags to riches

keep the noise to a minimal roar
pretend you can sleep
you're being looked at
by experts
they never really tell you what they're expert at
i guess we got to take their word
put some sunscreen on
might keep the fire at bay
drama in every bar of chocolate
rags and riches look the same
when a cloud climbs in your eye
the motel lobby is comfortable enough
it's time for me to go to the well with a bucket that
does not leak
keep the jail time to a dull roar.

emergency room of the stars

a brutal man confesses he's got a misunderstood soul
blame it all on the noise of the traffic
how the world lists from side to side
in the emergency room of the stars
all the doctors seem habitually young
the young french actresses climb the wall
the hallelujah boys and girls in heat
makes a tired man want to go swimming
the pond ducks on forever
god's playing stride piano
in a fancy house
bring all your toys inside
the first international bare foot
calmly squishes cities
makes a done-in man want to go on living
in the emergency room of the stars
the nurses have killed for love
bless them.

x

take your things inside

ugly men and women get lonely too
claimed the town crier
jesus never bragged about walking on water
it's a good job if you can get it
where do the happy people go
when the cops come calling
we all could use an island
my guardian angel got pulled over
the air here kind of thin
take your things inside
the sky is angry
a pianist will be here very soon
we'll measure one another
although numbers sometimes seem funny
my knees scrape hello
lift up your hand
ugly men and women goddamn photogenic
light enough to see, if you feel like it
i forgot my number
my body read your last book
i'll be here on the corner
the only job in town
shit washes off
sometimes
we congregate in the cheap seats
village elders battle alzheimer's
look to the moon
soon, your voice will re-create me
ugly men and women kiss
i'll be over by nine.

dakota lunch meat

the faithful swear they love you
all the doctors agree
soon i hear the revolution bust a gut
be wary of that old dakota lunch meat
sometimes the city asks for your hand
can't claim the name of such a planet
work me hard, snarled the incoming weather
i push my broom north across a bit of debris
the sooner-or-later boys
predict the award-winning actors
the fun house demands the noise get kept down
can't make out the country of your real name
swing state soft-shoe
only actual dance will know
the faithful cry out, they need you
all the undercover cops try to succeed
soon the exit jams up
be empathetic of that old dakota lunch meat
sometimes, you're the one
sometimes i feel a sun coming on
broke bugles still seek us
brokedown tunes will try to name us.

satisfied feeling

jesus christ lives in a homeless shelter
go and fetch him
the big game is coming up this weekend
the scouts feel he's got what it takes
the emergency room is full of satisfied feeling
and men and women who think they're big
i'm going to stay out late tonight
i heard tell a miracle was coming down
i frankly don't know what they look like
they might even be clowns
the renegade volcano tore through the living room
carpet
its lava means business
put something enduring into the coffee
lots of road ahead
all the religions of the world
running naked in the rain
hope nobody comes down with pneumonia
the sweet things show up after midnight
they are adept at throwing their voices
the heart all alone in some incorrigible desert
large enough to offer you a place to hide
the secret police are on their way
they look stunning in uniform
just a few of us pins standing
bowling never a strong suit
throw it hard, sweetie
the earth just delivered twins
jesus christ promises he'll drop in soon
he's catching up on his sleep
see me seeing you on the dance floor
i heard miracles pay their rent on time
paint the ceiling whatever color you damn well want.

143

crank her up

the giant saw me the other day
he's sick of being too big
want me to cut off your legs? i asked,
trying to be helpful
no thank you. i'll just have to live with being the
tallest man in the world
must be a bitch on planes, i suggested
king kong and fay wray live in retirement
sometimes the big ape gives me a call
king once was a slam poet of note
fay, on the other hand, has a quiet thing for
robert browning
crank her up, bobby, she sings
the casualty lists keep growing longer
is anybody home at headquarters?
the war heard this rumor about it. the rumor said,
you're done.
no matter where you swore you lived
a stretcher feels the same
crank yourself up, earth
the giant needs better socks
his toes ain't that pretty
tonight it's anyone's guess.

this prison sure be fine

william faulkner mississippi rain
come as you are
heard a not-too-funny story about a man and his dog
the price of gasoline
the prison claims it's fine
don't like the way the warden looks
raise your hands if you agree
some still call it democracy
where have our healers disappeared to?
not as far as you and me
slightly sweating under such a sun
it's time to pick up the wounded
nurses in attendance
walt whitman just about now
this prison will not disown us
words to that effect
minstrels begin to sing
stay as you are
satan has all the good drugs
they're carding god across the highway
all he's got on him is a learner's permit.

roll me over

lobotomies free for the first 100 people who show
roll me over baby and hang me out to dry
the commander-in-chief wet himself
santa claus had his shoes removed at the airport
my toilet backed up with dick cheney
the president's favorite star in a dual role in
rocky vs. rambo
pain on every corner
showing intimate snapshots
roll me down south
the big siesta will waken with a hangover
roll me sideways and unilateral
my bones are caucases full of comic books
court jester falls on his sword
robert oppenheimer on a skateboard
earth to god, what's it to you?
roll me up into something edible
saturday night all over the world
nobody home.

a storm might be coming

innocent men in prison, the new musical by
andrew lloyd webber
just moved in next door.
send them fine cookies to make you fat.
don't let the lawyers do the barbecue
they'll never agree when it's done.
the governor seems to enjoy sitting in the electric
chair.
he always was one well-grounded guy.
all nine supreme court justices
found crammed into a phone booth on a very dangerous
road.
you got to give it all your verve.
they beat up my guitar, the folk singer of renown
sings.
maybe we're outlaws
with difficult-sounding aliases.
dancing is a great exercise.
watch me leak through the keyhole.
a storm might be coming.
go ahead, pick yourself up, let's blow
that all-night music.
dogs come, dogs go
a few even got teeth.
raise your right hand tell nothing but.
the road goes straight north.
puny boys leave huge paw prints.
the earth pulled me under.
said i looked vaguely familiar.
i said, i danced at your wedding.
earth said, was i ever married?
something in the toothpaste, maybe.
the tone of voice they use when they read you your
rights.

weary river

it's time for all barefoot wonders to report in
they're adjusting the sky
televisions stare at us and wince
someone will be here soon with a yardstick
to see if we've measured up
strolling without a purpose is prohibited
guess that leaves my flat feet out
free countries are being given out at the telethon
you just have to prove your name and age
the last war just landed
after a long swim in weary river
this war is kind of pale
and can't tie its shoes
it'll kill you quick
in the good-old-days environment
orphans have many children
the traffic sometimes is too much
there must be a side street still in existence
a man kisses a saxophone
weary river will get you there
the barefoot wonders salute
you just have to remember your name and age.

wunderkind park

roll the bloody rock uphill
water boy, come super-quick
they're taking odds
summer could be real
mâitre d' eaten by food
an all-night set of footprints
adventure
once held up here
blended in with anything you can handle
soft beds on the camel's busted back
wunderkind park
a place to hobble
concertinas on fire in the sky
walk on broken glass barefoot.

Roast Beef Kill

Belly dancers slither across mashed potatoes
and gravy.
Sarcastic surgeons call in sick.
I wanted to fly without wings,
I wanted to hold my own,
but the killers shine younger with each fleeing hour.
I heard you were almost in town,
and my ears stood up in awe,
when your name smoked my brain
and all claimed it would be forgiven.
It's time to shed some skin and bludgeon my way out
onto the dance floor.
Mister music, please stop being deaf.
I wanted to get my vital statistics across,
but when I pulled the chain the water overflowed.
Some days the war just keeps humming.
Some nights you really don't know who you are.
I'd like to be in on the roast beef kill,
if the stars are lined up right.
The prison guards are getting younger,
and the master of ceremonies is wanted in six
different languages.
The brand-new superherculean building is built on a
mountain of garbage,
and toxins will be your best man at the wedding.
Deaf men and women make sloppy music critics,
and the blood slowly smiles as its rises.
I went outside to learn the address of oxygen,
I stumbled against the detonator.
They got a vital new jukebox
sitting out in the rain.
The A side is all-night thunder.
The B side disowns us.

I wanted to shimmy and shake.
I wanted to blow up the last balloon.
The advancing armies are here now
and lunatics will prevail.

where to go when your favorite hospital gets sick

there's a strange new group of people living in my icebox
if only they could be interesting
when i open it to get food
they go on and on about their troubles and woes
i don't mind troubles and woes in moderate amounts
all things in moderation the good book said
as for the bad book?
every time i try to get a copy at my local library, it's out
there are certain folks living among us
who figure their troubles are the only troubles in the world
i just need to vent, they say
they say it every morning, noon, and night
air used to come through the vent
but air once meant you could breathe
where do you go when your favorite hospital gets sick?
how many states can you name?
disregard ohio because that state flag apparently
stands for obama
i myself find many friends in the states of
confusion and chaos
maybe one of them actually got a copy of
the bad book in their local library
those strange new people in my icebox
would like to relocate to my microwave
they tire of the cold
and claim they understand heat
i guess we have to find out where our least favorite
hospital might live
the nurses there know how to party
i'd like to vent you my new book of love poems
i was going to kill off everyone in it
but i took a little bit longer under the shower

i realized that being a puny not-so-much human
was actually human and okay
they go on and on about improving our infrastructure
but those roads keep running short of the exit
walking's not all that bad
as long as your feet don't swell with water retention
last night a rhino charged
he tried to do american express
the international brotherhood of hooligans
has asked me to endorse somebody for something
i'd surely enjoy kicking you in the ass, said god
but i just pulled a leg muscle
i didn't want to waste too much of your time,
the traveling salesman said to the woman
at her wit's end
but i just wrote a screenplay
could i read it to you?
go ahead, then
pull the emergency stop
this train's been running in circles
by the time the antidote gets here
we'll have forgot just what poison we ingested
the all-night call-in-and-cry radio station
just picked up twelve new affiliates
i'm going to swing tree to tree with the monkeys
i'm going to learn a new trade
i'll cash in my chips soon
as soon as the face cards stop staring through me.

one night fits all

disappear into night
do it quiet
my head's gone off to foment revolution
my heart hangs around with domestic terrorists
the solar system is looking for a new medical plan
when we go to the racetrack
the horses refuse our bets
some of us, i guess, need to get lucky
some of us should maybe eventually get out of bed
santa claus is due in a couple of months
he's got some good new toys for the middle class
when you're in the middle of the class
it's equal distance to either the window or the door
which escape route is in your blood?
late last night eden got quarantined
some new obstreperous virus was discovered in the fruit
eve blamed adam
adam blamed god
god had no comment
it seemed he launched his campaign to make the world
in the living room of a known unrepentant felon
i wish the doctors would whisper louder
when they earnestly discuss our condition at cocktail
parties
the security boys load us up with every kind of stone
imaginable
now all we need is a glass house
my horror is bigger than your horror
and if it isn't, don't blame me for trying
one shoe fits all
even if your foot swells
a question of attitude
maybe even of purpose

i sort of got up this morning
i had nowhere to go
if i get there in time
it's anybody's game.

bye-bye sun

the sun got kidnapped
the sun done got swiped.
what can a poor fool hope to accomplish?
the library shelves are empty
the liquor bottles vacant.
call the plumber
get our coordinates mapped.
tell your mother to call back later.
the sun claimed it enjoyed our company
then took the next bus south.
christopher columbus' three means of transportation
hospital ships all.
mission control is in remission.
i'd love to walk with lovers.
i'd like to introduce you to my heart.
it just moves around way too fast.
i'm never sure where it's at.
i tell it to be home by six
but it never is.
i look up at the round hole in the sky
waiting for my cue.
i was eager three hours ago
but am told it'll take time.
authorities wait for a ransom note.
solar experts are all over the TV and radio.
the ultrasound is a little uncertain.
it gets that way sometimes.
i got into a long line.
i didn't know what the line was for
it just looked good.
you need to enjoy the good things.
a bad man once said that.
he said it so well i fell on the floor.

i might have got up
but that floor felt good.
when you lie on the floor
it seems your space is all that much bigger.

holding cell of love

seems lately the phone numbers i got are on the
endangered species list
when i go to make a call sirens get loud
am not so sure which of us knows how to dance
they swear they'll get you coming if not going
the rich and famous seen live wandering mangy streets
after curfew
trying to get a handle on it
the house keeps rising into the clouds
can't clarify what the roof can hold
debutantes on parole
walk the proud and narrow
make me happy, the dog panted
scratch my back as if it meant something
war heroes need a drink of water every now and then
sisyphus lives downhill these days
better when you park
holding cell of love
in every new town
the musicians always somehow different
but that damn song always runs right into you all the
same.

down and out

woke up upside down
the blood was rushing to my head in major disagreement
rock slides everywhere
even in places where no rocks ever picked up their mail
going down the proverbial line
going to hang my seditious laundry in public
king kong tells dr. phil he can't understand why
ann darrow left him
i was a good provider, he sobs
good providers all over the slumping planet
find themselves waiting for a bus that is hours overdue
the spanish armada finally resurfaced after all these years
we were down and out, all those ships mumble
sir francis drake was a cold number
all the cold numbers are going to be played tonight
grab your warm dancing partner and be prepared to atone
i ran outside when the atone wagon pulled through my
part of town
i had enough change to buy some peace of mind
on a sliding scale, mind you
people can't afford to gamble in this scary economy
hope they don't have to turn off the night neon in vegas
all those colors make the place seem palatable
the worse-for-wear universal rag band
is cutting a brand-new record
so many scratches on the CD
so many holes in the dam
all that repressed water is going to vent very soon
get yourself a waterproof way of being
went to bed inside out
events were making too much noise in my bones
the ability to fly gets kind of weary
luca brasi still sleeps with the fishes

i saw him hanging with mr. limpet and moby dick
down and out is my new P.O. box address
send all care packages book rate, it's cheaper
the lost stumble around the depot
the last train to clarity is about to pull out
wave your ticket at the wolf pack
they just might let you get on
down and out checked into the hospital
the birth was a success . . . twins!
my newspaper read me and winced
guess it'll cancel its subscription
henry miller and little red riding hood
went out walking one day
would you like something to eat, mr.miller? red asked
my mouth is wide open, red
mussolini tried to make my toy train run on time
he died and nobody wept
down and out just moved in next door
i'll try to keep my life's tendency to make noise
to a minimum
i fall out of bed and discover fred c. dobbs looking for the
mother of all lodes
put some strong anything on.

let everybody come in

i'm too dense and stupid, i suppose
to understand the rabid hatred and fear people have for
people they
don't know
relationships are difficult countries
you file your citizenship papers and hope the best
in a world of killing and war
how can love be an evil?
doesn't matter if the love is between a man and a woman
certainly doesn't matter if it's between a man and a man
or a woman and a woman
love is just too damn hard to find
on a planet bent on ethnic cleansing, racial hatred, and
murderous intent
in the name of whatever god you break bread with
one should bow down, applaud, when love walks by
the heart is a torn planet
spinning out of control at times
i'm just too dense and stupid, i suppose
when hate-filled fearful people tell me god wants certain
humans to go to hell
for following their hearts
they claim they read it all in some best-selling book
man shall not lay with man
they snap
somewhere in the same book
guess it depends on your translation
it says do not kill and love your neighbor
okay, i guess the book is schizo and uneven
maybe it needs editing and clarifying
is god ahab bent on harpooning all humans that look to
him like moby dick?
or is god the daddy of jesus who said you gotta give it
up and love

can god give it up and love?
ye shall not do this and that
if i see two men or women in love
it makes my wornout heart smile
let everybody into the party
it's not going to be going on forever
ye shall pull back your venom
ye shall examine your own spirit
have anger, fear, and hate gnawed on you enough
that you've become a shrill foghorn in the opaque night
dan white killed harvey milk and george moscone
in a city reportedly famous for its tolerance
they said twinkies were the reason
in that book these angry people keep referring to
it says nothing about twinkies giving you the right to kill
others
later dan white would kill himself
harvey milk, george moscone, and dan white deserved to
live to be old toothless hermits
wandering the lost highways of our weaving lives
it's time to find a better book
a book that condemns none for being true to themselves
and their feelings

god, i guess, created psychiatrists
because poor humans have difficulty in their feelings
i'm too dense and stupid, i know
but people in love give our species hope
a man has a right to love a man
a woman has a right to love a woman
i never read any book that said love was evil
if i did, i'd send it back to the publisher and ask for a refund
everybody can come to the dance
the band will implode soon enough
there are a thousand and one ways to hate and die every
day
if you see love, jump for joy and shout as loud as you can

you might not see it again for a long time
when you're done reading this ramble
reach out to the one you love and sing them a song
if you haven't anyone to love
sing to yourself
sing it loud
and deny books that preach hate and violence
no matter its position on the bestseller list
i'm dense and stupid and empathetic and goofy
as i bump against the walls
singing
mostly john prine a cappella
the heart is a torn planet
it needs mending daily
this poem goes out to all lovers
heterosexual, homosexual, lesbian
love comes, goes, builds a house, runs away
the species rolls across the earth
i guess you could call it exercise
exercise the heart
be who you are
rock hudson had to live a double life
it's hard enough living one life
no more reasons to cover yourself up under the tarp
the rain may be coming down
raise yourself up and feel it on your face
nobody can truly plan the weather for tomorrow
but i want to see you out there
bopping to the rhythm section of your soul.

moodswing hotel

welcome to moodswing hotel
every second an emotional surprise
you never know what you'll be dealing with
sometimes the inmates are jovial and say hello
sometimes their faces are granite
there are conference rooms full of sobbing dignitaries
you can even gamble in the nothing-is-guaranteed room
one crisp morning i locked myself out of my room
i wasn't ready to confront the world
i froze in the hallway
my ABCs were rusty
my ability to discern reality from my interior indulgences
at an all-time low
a golden retriever walking a blind girl on a leash
stopped by and was about to lift its leg
hold on, i said, i'm not him
the retriever, satisfied, lowered his leg and walked on
god bless you for not being him, the blind girl shouted
the trouble was i could very well
have been him but just forgot
my identity was locked in my room
i stood in front of a vending machine
staring at what i looked like
am i him indeed?
and just who in the hell is him?
some years hence they'll be sitting around the main stem
talking not much of anything
working their jaws just to see if they still apply
and they'll say,
oh, him . . . we remember him too damn well
i went into the take-a-chance dining room
how many in your party? i got asked
anybody who wants it, i said
my door is always open.

our special today is eggs sunny-side amnesiac,
my waitress said
the more you stuff yourself, the more you forget
is memory that bad? i asked
depends on how much you need to lose, she smiled
i tried to figure just how much i needed to lose
or if on any given day i just might win
all that figuring gave me a headache
moods swinging from high trees
they need cutting down
the landscape drives, at times, too hard a bargain.

what i want for my 56th birthday

mad men and women to get their fair share
bank presidents follow horses in parades and clean up
their stories
hungry people open well-received restaurants
poets form a union (it'll never happen, we're too contrary)
the dance, despite its anemia, doddering steps, and
scarred skin
to continue to upset the equilibrium
what i want for my 56th
is for all of you to hang on
the ceiling is leaking
the landlord is on a permanent vacation
hold onto your flotation device
the sea is a bit angry
but it has an appointment with its counselor next week
all of you teach me to hobble upright
all of you glow in the impenetrable dark
sometimes my ability to hear is full of wax
i still feel your rhythms
together we survive the deluge
together we topple the nasty gods
i know we are imperfect, not that stable, and wondrously
ridiculous
it's what makes us endurable
for my 56th i invite you to keep enduring
the size of the falling rocks gets bigger every year
and the carport is full of wreckage
hold on and if you feel yourself slipping
i'll come running with the flimsy band-aid and iodine
i really don't want anything for my 56th
except for you to keep singing and yelling
in my face
it makes the day take a second look

it makes the night dream a little more rhythmic
it'll take time for the sutures of humans to become
new forests
let's go swinging from limb to limb
sometimes we'll fall
and land in a mine field
relax, breathe easy, those mines have amnesia
they forgot their chosen roles in all of this
we get up and hurl ourselves against the incoming
hordes
then it's time for standing on our heads
and mumbling new countries of grunts
for my 56th i ask you to grunt in unison
it has such a perfect pitch
the maestro swoons and the no-trespassing signs
burn up.

luminous possibility

luminous possibility is up for an academy award
it tore everyone up in its performance
most everyone crawled out of the theater, shaking
themselves
if only they could read the small print on the label
my reading glasses tried and shattered
i'm not adept at crawling these days
my legs, knees, and thighs are too cranky
luminous possibility got caught crossing the state line
with an underage girl
it claimed she seduced it
the arresting officers somehow weren't moved
the house you're moving into has a controversial
foundation
rumors abound it was tempted to pay for obama's senate
seat
i once caught a rumor pouring sugar into your gas tank
luminous possibility blackmailed me into doing it,
rumor cried
when you see a rumor hustling across the floor
you tend to smash it with your foot
i hear you were calm and serene in your backyard garden
when a man-eating plant snapped you up
the lord works in mysterious ways, the chimpanzees sing
somebody go solve a crime
or turn some dancing music on
sometimes this planet's a morgue
tell room service to send up something endearing
the authorities gave luminous possibility a lethal
injection
luminous began to quote rudyard kipling's "if"
tell the bus driver i meant the next stop
if there truly is one.